The Complete Guide to

Bearded Dragon Care and Ownership

Alisha Cuarenta

LP Media Inc. Publishing
Text copyright © 2023 by LP Media Inc.

Publication Data

Alisha Cuarenta
The Complete Guide to Bearded Dragon Care and Ownership – First edition.
Summary: "Successfully caring for and owning a Bearded Dragon"
Provided by publisher.
ISBN: 978-1-954288-97-3
[1. The Complete Guide to Bearded Dragon Care and Ownership – Non-Fiction] I. Title.

Design by Sorin Rădulescu
First paperback edition, 2023

TABLE OF CONTENTS

INTRODUCTION

Chapter 1

Chapter 2

Chapter 3

INTRODUCTION

When first hearing about the possibility of owning a bearded dragon as a pet, many people become intimidated, especially those who have never owned a reptile before. Owning an exotic reptile, such as a bearded dragon, doesn't have to be scary or intimidating. These social, curious, friendly, but, at times, feisty reptiles make for excellent pets for anyone willing to put in the work and time. While caring for a bearded dragon does require specialized care, don't let the words "exotic" or "reptile" stop you from experiencing one.

Years ago, when my oldest son was three years old, his interest in reptiles sparked. That spark lit a fire within him, and his fascination and passion for them intensified over the next few years. Reptiles have never frightened me, but what did was my gut feeling he would want one as a pet someday. Unsurprisingly, I was right. When he turned seven, he asked me if he could have a reptile.

Instantly, my mind swirled with uncertainty and hesitation, for I had always preferred and was familiar with "the warm and fuzzy." The what-ifs plagued me, and the fear of the unknown and my limited reptile knowledge kept me in my comfort zone. As time continued, my son remained adamant about wanting a reptile to care for, so reluctantly, I agreed to explore the world of reptiles with him. Together, we learned a lot about them and the care they required, and because of that, my fears melted, and the what-ifs slowly dissipated.

As more time passed, my calloused heart softened to the possibility of having a reptile for a pet, and I was now ready to take the leap. When my son turned eight, we became the proud owners of our first reptile, Owen, an eight-week-old bearded dragon. In short, it has been a learning experience, an adventure, and a complete blast. Whether you have just begun to consider a bearded dragon for a pet, have just gotten one, or want to freshen up your knowledge, this book is here to give you helpful, practical, and easy-to-understand information.

CHAPTER 1

Introduction to Bearded Dragons

> 66
>
> *Bearded dragons make excellent pets for first-time reptile owners. They are our most popular reptile, and we sell several hundred a year to owners from families with children as young as three or four, all the way up to grandparents in their seventies and eighties! They are rewarding reptiles to keep—active, inquisitive, interesting to watch, and, having kept and bred so many over the years, I can definitely say they have different personalities too.*
>
> CHRISTY BRUCKNER
>
> *Reptile Cymru*
>
> 99

The reptile world is a fascinating one, indeed. Although some would never dare to open the door to this world, for the thought of owning such a creature sends chills down their spine, reptile lovers could never live without one. There are many reptiles available that make great pets. Of those reptiles, bearded dragons, also called "dragons" or "beardies," often steal the spotlight and catch the eye of anyone who looks in their direction. With their cute, dragon-like appearance and friendly disposition, it is no wonder bearded dragons continue to top the charts as one of the most popular reptiles owned.

Photo Courtesy of
Aliesha Dean
Wrathgate Reptiles

Description and History

There are more than 6000 species of lizards in the world, eight of which are bearded dragons, all originating in Australia. Of these eight species, the Inland, or Central bearded dragon, is the most common species bought, bred, sold, and found in Australia. Scientifically named Pogona vitticeps, this species is the best choice for first-time reptile owners because of its very docile and calm temperament. The Pogona vitticeps species will be focused on throughout this book.

Physical Characteristics

Bearded dragons are cold-blooded reptiles covered with and pro-tected by dry, spiny reptilian scales. These medium-sized lizards average 16 to 24 inches in length, having tails usually just as long as their heads and bodies. They can live anywhere from eight to 15 years in captivity, with

10 years being the average. In the wild, they are dust-colored, tan, or dull brown with orange, yellow, or red highlights.

Bearded dragons belong to the Pogona genus family, stemming from the Greek word pogon, meaning "beard." A "beard" can be found on the throat that flares out and may blacken depending on their mood. Spikes exist on their oversized head and throat and line both sides of their lower body. All bearded dragons have broad, flat bodies and strong, stocky legs. As a result, they can run up to an astonishing nine miles per hour, which is handy when seeing a hawk's shadow. They can sense the shadow with the "third eye" located on top of the head, called the parietal eye.

Behaviors

In their natural habitat, bearded dragons situate themselves on rocks, fallen timber, stumps, and low-lying branches when basking, napping, or surveying the landscape for potential danger. They are challenging to spot due to their remarkable ability to hide and blend into their surroundings. Furthermore, since they are diurnal animals, they are active during the day and sleep at night. Throughout the day, they know how to position themselves perfectly, making adjustments to regulate their body temperature as necessary.

When bearded dragons achieve their optimal temperature, they move silently through the environment, looking for insects, vegetation, and even small mammals to devour. They ambush their prey with intense drive and focus when they spot it. If a chase is necessary, bearded

Photo Courtesy of
Brian Meers

dragons thoroughly enjoy trailing ever so closely behind their meal. They use their sticky tongues and strong jaws to crush prey and swallow it in a few bites.

Bearded dragons mainly live solitary lives, and although not social, when unthreatened, they quietly communicate their mood and intent to nearby bearded dragons using color display, methodical limb movements, head bobbing, beard flaring, and different postures. A male and female come in contact with each other only to mate, and males only

FUN FACT

A Docile Lizard

Despite their fearsome name and appearance, bearded dragons are very social, friendly, and docile pets. These gentle reptiles are easy to tame and handle if appropriately socialized. Some owners even claim their bearded dragons can recognize them by sight or scent.

meet with other males to fight for territory, food, or to compete for a female. Extremely aggressive and territorial toward other bearded dragons, they fight with the intent to injure and kill their opponents. They will use techniques such as beard inflation, blackening of the beard, hissing, chin raising, and aggressive biting when threatened or defending what is theirs.

Natural Habitat

Bearded dragons inhabit most of Australia in the wild. They thrive in warm, dry climates and can be found in scrubland, savannas, subtropical woodlands, and deserts. Semi-arboreal and great climbers, they idle on top of roadside fences, posts, fallen branches, and trees. In addition, they burrow underground to escape the extreme heat of Australia and predators.

History in the Pet Trade

The export or import of any plant or animal became prohibited nationally by law in Australia in the 1960s. To this day, exactly how bearded dragons ended up permanently in the pet trade market worldwide is not fully understood. Some speculate that even after the complete ban was executed by the Australian government, somewhere between the mid-1970s and 1990s, people were still smuggling bearded dragons out of Australia to other countries. Within that short time frame, it didn't take long for bearded dragons to become highly in demand and for captive breeding to take a foothold.

Why Choose a Bearded Dragon?

> 66
>
> *Bearded dragons make excellent pets even for first-time owners. They're docile, low-key, very gentle and friendly, and also kind of funny. When you deal with them on a day-to-day basis, maintenance is very minimal. Plus, they like human interaction very much.*
>
> FRANCISCO E. AQUINO SANCHEZ
>
> *Rhegal Dragons*
>
> 99

There are numerous reasons to choose a bearded dragon as a pet. From their friendly, gentle, and tame temperaments and ability to bond with their owner to their responsive and interactive personality and simple care, bearded dragons make very satisfying pets for both the young and old. Not only do they happen to be intelligent, but they also happen to be quite beautiful too. As you can see, it's no surprise they have taken the world by storm in number and popularity.

Photo Courtesy of Alyssa Vargas

Low Maintenance

A bearded dragon is considered a low-maintenance pet and one of the easiest reptiles to own. It requires minimal daily care that you can complete within 10 minutes or less. Unlike a dog or cat, it doesn't shed all over your house, which is favorable for people with pet allergies. It also doesn't require excessive interaction, frequent vet trips, or a rigorous exercise regimen. After doing your part to learn the proper way to care for your dragon, you will find it quite simple, especially once you get into the swing of things.

Bonds with Owner

As strange as it may sound, bearded dragons can bond closely with their owners. When handled and interacted with properly, they enjoy being held and petted. Since they are relatively calm and rarely bite, handling them is fun. Lovingly deemed "lap lizards," bearded dragons cuddle on the laps of their owners, similar to the way a cat would. They can bond with family members through activities, treats, toys, and more.

Opportunity to Learn and Interact

Owning a bearded dragon allows you to learn about and interact with an exotic lizard. Even though bearded dragons are becoming increasingly popular, they are still less common than other pets. Our bearded dragon has bridged the gap between reptiles and humans by being the first dragon many of our extended family and friends have experienced. He has received mixed reviews from those who have met him; some have been amazed, some a little unsure, and some have been terrified—but only at first—mainly because they had no prior bearded dragon knowledge or interaction.

Choosing the Right Lizard

Bringing a new bearded dragon into your life is an exciting affair. However, there are some crucial factors you need to consider and decide on before you set out to get your dragon. It can be overwhelming to pick out the right dragon that best suits you and your preferences if you don't know what you are doing. This section will help you gather the necessary information to weigh your options to make choosing the right bearded dragon easier.

Types of Bearded Dragons

You can select a different type of bearded dragon species, morph, or color if you so desire. Various morphs and colors are available, but only a few species are permitted as pets. Maybe you will want to keep it simple and get a classic bearded dragon, or perhaps you'll want an even more unique dragon by choosing one with a mutation to its scales or a vibrant color. Whichever you choose, you will love your new pet all the same.

Species

Each sun-loving bearded dragon species originates from a slightly different habitat in Australia. They have similarities in appearance and behavior that make them recognizable as bearded dragons, but each species has unique qualities that set it apart. The Inland or Central bearded dragon is the most common species kept, with the Rankin's bearded dragon coming in second. The following are the eight species of bearded dragons.

1. Central bearded dragon (Pogona vitticeps)
2. Rankin's bearded dragon (Pogona henrylawsoni)
3. Eastern bearded dragon (Pogona barbata)
4. North-West bearded dragon (Pogona mitchelli)
5. Kimberley bearded dragon (Pogona microlepidota)

6. Abrolhos Dwarf bearded dragon (Pogona minor minima)
7. Dwarf bearded dragon (Pogona minor minor)
8. Nullarbor bearded dragon (Pogona nullarbor)

Central bearded dragon
(Pogona vitticeps)

Rankin's bearded dragon
(Pogona henrylawsoni)

Eastern bearded dragon
(Pogona barbata)

North-West bearded dragon
(Pogona mitchelli)

Abrolhos Dwarf bearded dragon
(Pogona minor minima)

Dwarf bearded dragon
(Pogona minor minor)

Morph Variety

There are many different kinds of bearded dragon morphs available in captivity. The term "morph" refers to a bearded dragon with one or more unique traits or characteristics that differ from the bearded dragons found in the wild. Breeders create and refine morphs by handpicking particular recessive and dominant genes in a male and female dragon to pass down to their offspring. Recessive and dominant genes can affect the bearded dragon's overall appearance, like its body type, scales, and size. The rare and more desirable dragon morphs come at a much higher price. The following are some, but not all, of the most popular bearded dragon morphs available.

Classic Morph

Classic morphs, also called standard or normal morphs, are bearded dragons that look most like the ones found in the wild. Their bodies have flat spiny scales and spikes on their beards and sides, and they have large triangular-shaped heads. Their scales have  an organized and consistent arrangement and can form striped patterns along their backs and tails. Lastly, classic morphs have eyes that are yellow or brown, and they have a dark streak that runs through the length of their claws.

German Giant Morph

German giant morphs are the largest bearded dragons available in the pet trade. As the name suggests, these "giants" can reach 30 inches when fully grown. They differ from other morphs by having much larger bodies with proportionally smaller heads. Unlike the classic

morph's yellow eyes, they have silvery or gold eyes instead. Considering that they are much bigger, a larger enclosure will be necessary.

Leatherback Morph

Leatherback dragons look and feel different than other bearded dragons because they have smooth backs and feel softer. Their smooth backs result from a mutation that causes the spiny scales on their backs to be absent. However, they will still have spikes on the sides of their bodies and heads, although not as protruding as classic bearded dragons' spikes. Furthermore, the missing spiny scales can also cause the coloration to appear brighter and more vivid than other bearded dragons.

Silkback or Scaleless Morph

Silkback morphs, also called scaleless morphs or silkies, are soft and smooth, with no scales or spikes anywhere on their bodies. The absence of scales and spikes gives them a look that resembles amphibians more than reptiles. For the same reason as leatherback morphs, they, too, appear more vivid. Compared to other morphs, they require more intensive and attentive care and are easier to injure. It should be pointed out that many passionate breeders find breeding silkies unethical because of the many problems the lack of scales and spikes can generate.

Dunner Morph

At first glance, dunner morphs appear very similar to classic morphs, but upon closer look, there are many differences worth mentioning. Dunner morphs have cone-shaped scales instead of tear-drop-shaped scales like classic morphs have. In addition, their 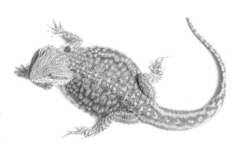 cone-shaped scales appear unorganized and not arranged in any particular pattern. Furthermore, contrary to the classic morph's spikes that point downward, the spikes on the dunner morph's beards point to the sides. They often have randomized spots on their backs and tails that differ in size instead of the classic morph's stripes. They have noticeably longer feet, claws, and broader tails. The dunner's distinctive traits contribute to their less smooth, more rugged, and primitive appearance.

Hypomelanistic Morph

Hypomelanistic morphs, called hypos for short, are intentionally bred to have low melanin or dark pigmentation in their skin, scales, eyes, and claws. The reduced levels of melanin in their scales help the other light colors appear more vibrant. Although at first, when they are born, they are often brightly colored, as they  mature, their color gradually subsides to a paler color because of the below-average levels of melanin. The final result is a light-colored adult bearded dragon with reduced dark patterns and clear claws.

Zero Morph

The Zero morph is a relatively new morph of the bearded dragon with a fascinating appearance. They don't have the usual pattern and pigmentation that classic bearded dragons display due to the scale mutation that results in their bodies being completely patternless. Furthermore, they also have substantially reduced, but not absent, melanin. Therefore, they have pale solid-colored bodies that range  from silver to dark gray and can also have light-colored patches near their shoulders.

Witblits Morph

Witblits morphs originated from south Africa and are another type of patternless bearded dragon with very minimal markings. Witblits morphs are one solid, uniform color and can be pale gray, dull earth, or pastel. They are commonly mistaken for zero morphs,  but unlike zero morphs, they have no color on their shoulders. Since they are relatively new, they are pretty expensive to buy.

Wero Morph

Wero morphs are created by cross-breeding zero morphs with witblits morphs. They are pale-colored—sometimes very close to white—and appear patternless. They look similar to zeros, except they have a few darker patches on their back or around the base of the tail. Weros differ from witblits morphs because they cannot hold color in their scales. They are also relatively new, rare, and highly sought after, making them costly.

Translucent Morph

Translucent morphs, trans for short, are born with thin semi-transparent skin and scales. As a result, their internal organs are semi-visible, giving their bellies a blue appearance. Likewise, they can also have dark

black eyes with blue eyelids. As they develop, their skin thickens, reducing their transparent look, and their black eyes sometimes revert to the color of classic bearded dragon's eyes. As adults, they end up being lighter in color overall.

Color Variants

Through selective breeding, breeders have created many richly-colored bearded dragons that are an option for you to select. Breeders take, for instance, the reddest dragon from one clutch and breed it with a similarly colored dragon from another. They repeat the process until the desired color is achieved: a bright red dragon. Breeders apply the same method to achieve colors such as orange, tan, white, gray, green, blue, and more. Varying shades of each color are available.

Factors to Consider When Choosing a Bearded Dragon

> 66
>
> *Unlike many other pets, bearded dragons need absolutely no friends. In fact, they are solitary animals and prefer to live in solitude. Especially for beginners, we recommend one bearded dragon per terrarium.*
>
> RENZO
>
> *OlympicBeardedDragon*
>
>

A bearded dragon makes for a very rewarding pet, but it is a long-term commitment that deserves careful thought. As with all pets, you will want to consider a couple of factors before buying your dragon. By considering essential elements, such as age, gender, size, and personality, you will be best prepared, setting yourself up for success. In addition, considering these factors allows you to fine-tune and customize the care and the enclosure to your specific dragon.

Consider Age

When choosing a bearded dragon, one factor to consider is whether to get a hatchling, baby, juvenile, or adult dragon. Having an age in mind will help you know the appropriate equipment, supplies, and care needed. There are a lot of conflicting opinions about what age is best for a first-time bearded dragon owner. Most experts agree that the older, the better, and suggest a dragon at least six months old.

Photo Courtesy of Kendra Cummings

Older dragons have a great deal of resilience, recovering well from possible mistakes made by inexperienced first-time bearded dragon owners. However, if you prefer to start with a younger dragon, it should be at least six weeks old or six to eight inches long. First-time bearded dragon owners shouldn't purchase a hatchling. Although adorable, hatchlings are at a vulnerable age where they are fragile and less resilient than older dragons.

Consider Male vs. Female

Most people will have to wait until their baby bearded dragon is at least four to six months old to be able to tell if it's a male or female. If you are getting an older dragon and aren't sure which sex to choose, you should know that they look and act very similar but have some differences. For instance, male dragons tend to be larger and have bigger heads, beards, and fatter tails than females. They also are a lot more territorial towards other dragons. Something worth considering is that females will lay infertile eggs even if no male is present.

Consider Personality

You will want to select a bearded dragon with a good personality since your new pet will be with you for a decade or more. If possible, asking to handle the bearded dragon is one of the best ways to see its character. The dragon should be alert, curious, and active. While a dragon with an "aggressive" and healthy appetite is considered a positive quality, a bearded dragon with an aggressive personality is a negative one. If the dragon you're looking at has its mouth wide open, its beard puffed out, and it is trying to bite, look at getting a different one.

Consider Size

Another factor to consider is the size of a bearded dragon. Bearded dragons grow rapidly and will be about 16 to 24 inches in length by the time they are fully grown at 16 to 18 months. Although not large lizards, adult dragons need at least a 40-gallon enclosure. The bigger the enclosure size, the better. Whichever enclosure size you choose, ensure you have space inside your home to accommodate it. The following approximate measurements of specific enclosure sizes are listed for reference.

Enclosure Size (in gallons)	Approximate Measurements (in inches)
20	30 x 12 x 12
40	30 x 18 x 18
55	48 x 13 x 21
75	48 x 18 x 21
120	48 x 24 x 24

Tips for Finding a Reputable Breeder or Pet Store

> **"**
>
> *It's important to try to buy from someone who knows the bearded dragon's history and has chosen to breed from healthy adults, then raised the hatchlings from birth on the correct diet and in the correct setup. Whether this is a breeder or a pet store is not that important in my mind, as long as the pet store is doing the breeding itself. There are unwelcome genetic traits in bearded dragons, and breeders will find some adults simply do not produce the healthiest or the best offspring. A responsible breeder will know the full history and only breed for good health.*
>
> CHRISTY BRUCKNER
> *Reptile Cymru*
> **"**

You will want to put a reasonable amount of time into researching and finding someone who will be able to produce a happy, thriving, and healthy bearded dragon for you. Finding someone you trust is the beginning to finding your new pet. Will you buy your dragon from a breeder? Pet store? Rescue? Or a private party? No matter your choice, you will want to take the necessary precautions and steps to find a high-quality dragon.

Local Breeder

Local breeders possess an abundance of valuable knowledge and experience. They will be able to answer your many questions or concerns and assist you along the way. Breeders often carefully pair specific bearded dragons with particular aspects in mind to produce high-quality offspring. You may be able to find a local breeder by word of mouth, on a reptile forum, through reptile magazines, in the newspaper, or through your local herpetological society. A reputable and respected breeder will be friendly and knowledgeable and promptly return your calls, texts, or emails. If they are impatient, hard to get a hold of, or have little knowledge about bearded dragons, keep searching.

Online Breeder

Another option is to find a reputable online breeder who can ship a bearded dragon by mail. You can find breeders online through search engines, word of mouth, bearded dragon forums, or by contacting your local herpetological society. A reputable breeder will have accurate and abundant bearded dragon knowledge, including how to swiftly and safely ship your dragon in the mail. When selecting online breeders, check out their reviews, as they should have plenty of positive and consistent reviews. A reputable breeder will be easy to get a hold of and happy to answer any questions.

You will not be able to see your bearded dragon personally if you purchase it from an online breeder. However, a reputable online breeder should have multiple pictures of the dragon from all angles for you to view. Since you won't see your dragon in person, you are responsible for getting the best impression of the bearded dragon through the pictures. Details on how to choose a healthy bearded dragon are discussed shortly in this chapter.

Pet Stores

Many pet stores have a selection of reptiles in stock readily available, including bearded dragons, that you can see up close and personal. A good pet store should be clean and have healthy animals with clean enclosures and adequate food and water. They will also have employees who know the ins and outs of each animal in their care, can answer your questions accurately, and provide the appropriate supplies and products for your new pet. Something worth remembering is that some pet stores will not allow you to buy a new enclosure and your bearded dragon at the same time. They will require you to have the enclosure setup before you bring your dragon home to make the transition as smooth and stress-free as possible.

Rescue

Sometimes bearded dragons are obtainable through animal rescues and private parties. A quick Google search will guide you to local reptile rescue organizations in your area. If you want to rescue a bearded dragon from an animal rescue or a private party, you should ask many questions to understand how it has been raised. You will want to ensure it's healthy because a sick dragon is best left to an experienced individual. Nonetheless, sometimes a bearded dragon's history remains unknown. In this case, you will need to examine the dragon thoroughly, as its physical state will be the only way to tell if it's healthy.

Selecting a Healthy Dragon

> **"**
>
> *It is important that the bearded dragon you choose is alert. Furthermore, you should obviously have a good feeling about it; it is a pet that you are likely to keep for a long time.*
>
> RENZO
>
> *OlympicBeardedDragon*
>
> **"**

No matter where you get your bearded dragon, there are specific indicators to look for to find the healthiest dragon. A healthy dragon has bright, clear, alert eyes, an attentive expression, and a good posture. Furthermore, a healthy dragon is neither skinny nor has any visible bones, and it should have fat deposited at the base of its tail. It is not uncommon for bearded dragon babies to bite or nip at each other, sometimes amputating toes and tail tips. Confirm that it has all five toes with claws on all four feet and a full tail. Make sure no body parts are swollen or deformed.

If you are able to see the dragon in person, examine the bearded dragon to ensure it has good skin texture, is free of lumps or lacerations, and has a nose clear of any mucus. Turn the dragon over to make sure

*Photo Courtesy of
Gustav Smedegard*

no fecal matter is stuck on it. If it shows all the signs of being a healthy dragon, ask if feeding the bearded dragon in front of you is possible. Watching the dragon eat is an excellent way to see which dragons have aggressive and healthy appetites for insects and leafy greens.

CHAPTER 2

Housing and Environment

> *Always give your dragon as much space as possible, as well as the best equipment and the best care. Don't go by minimum guidelines. It's critical that a new owner has a full setup that is an appropriate size, with correct heating and lighting. Any responsible seller will not sell unless you have this. Additional items you might need could include feeding tongs for hand-feeding live food, a tap water conditioner, or even a harness and leash for taking your dragon for a walk. Always strive to provide the very best and you'll have a dragon that is healthy and happy.*
>
> CHRISTY BRUCKNER
>
> *Reptile Cymru*

Imagine a bearded dragon in the Australian outback: the air is hot and arid, and the temperature is climbing to a sizzling degree. Yet, the bearded dragon is thriving in its element. Having boundless barren terrain, it instinctively shifts in and out of the heat to maintain a perfect internal temperature. It moves to a location with more shade when it gets too hot and to the ideal spot to bask and soak in some rays when it is cold. It can bask, lounge, explore, and hide as it pleases. The goal is to recreate this natural habitat in your captive dragon's enclosure. Considering that reptile enclosure decorations, furniture, and supplies have advanced, you might be amazed at how close you can get.

Setting Up a Suitable Habitat

> " *We recommend a minimum of a forty-gallon breeder enclosure with measurements of at least 36x18x18, with branches, logs, and a cave for them to climb on, sleep in, and lounge or bask on. For a substrate, we use reptile carpet, and keep several on hand for quick cleaning.*
>
> MARK DOHMEN AND KATIE GROVE
> *Midwest Dragons* "

Creating the ideal enclosure for your bearded dragon can be a lot of fun. It involves a little trial and error and a lot of learning and patience. You will want to provide your bearded dragon with a spacious habitat where it can freely behave just like it would in the wild—a place where it can do all the things dragons do naturally. You can make the enclosure as elaborate as you would like. Make sure you set up the enclosure correctly before getting your dragon.

Size

A baby dragon can benefit from starting in a smaller 20-gallon enclosure instead of a 40-gallon if your budget allows it. A smaller enclosure can reduce stress for your dragon and make finding its food easier. As the dragon grows, a bigger enclosure will be necessary. However, many start

DID YOU KNOW?
Beardies for Short

Bearded dragons are affectionately called "beardies" by enthusiasts and owners of these unique reptiles. Speaking of names, some bearded dragon owners report that their lizards can learn to recognize their names and answer when called. In addition, some bearded dragons are so intelligent that they can learn to respond to several short and simple verbal commands.

with a larger enclosure because it's cost-effective, and the baby dragons do just fine.

When a bearded dragon is fully grown, it will need a minimum enclosure size of 40 gallons. Many consider a 40-gallon enclosure for a dragon to be a tight living space, but it would get you by. A 75-gallon enclosure or bigger is ideal. Pet store owner and bearded dragon breeder Christy Buckner says, *"Always give your dragon as much space as possible, the best equipment, and the best care. Don't go by the minimum guidelines. Always strive to provide the very best, and you'll have a dragon that is healthy and happy."* Below is the minimum enclosure size required specific to your bearded dragon's age.

Age	Enclosure Size
Baby	20 gallon
Juvenile	40 gallon
Adult	40+ gallon
Adult (20+ inches)	75+ gallon

Type

Many types of enclosures are available to house your bearded dragon. They range from practical to advanced, with some so visually appealing they look like a piece of artwork in your home. Bearded dragon enclosures come in three primary materials: glass, plastic, and wood. Enclosures range in price significantly, and it's best first to decide how much you are willing to spend and then find one that fits your budget. The best enclosures will have good ventilation, withstand high temperatures, and be spacious.

Glass Enclosures

Glass enclosures are the most popular choice because of their price and accessibility. Sleek and modern-looking glass vivariums are one type of glass enclosure available. They have front-facing doors, making access

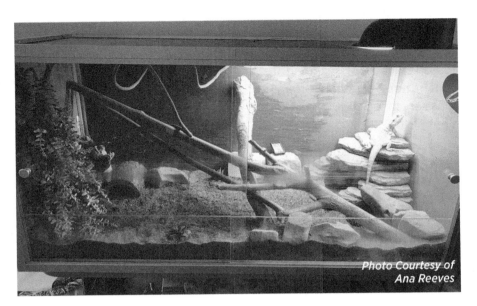

Photo Courtesy of Ana Reeves

to inside the enclosure and dragon easy and convenient. They are usually made of low-reflectivity glass that is easy to clean and scratch-resistant.

The other kind of glass enclosure looks nearly identical to an aquarium. These glass enclosures are easy to clean, durable, scratch-resistant, and offer excellent visibility. Unfortunately, they don't have convenient front-facing doors. They are also much heavier and have poorer insulation and heat retention when compared to wood or plastic enclosures. If you purchase a glass enclosure, make sure there is a cover. The cover should be a durable mesh screen, never glass, that allows suitable ventilation and permits humidity to escape and light to pass through.

Plastic Enclosures

Plastic enclosures have greatly improved over the years, with many stylish options, colors, and convenient features now available. Plastic enclosures are made from premade molded plastic and have convenient front-facing doors. They are lightweight, stackable, durable, and water-resistant. You can't see through the sides or the top of the enclosure, providing bearded dragons with an extra sense of security. Plastic enclosures hold heat effectively, but the airflow is not as good as in glass enclosures, so be sure to check the humidity levels often. Cost-wise, they are much more expensive than a glass enclosure.

FUN FACT
What's in a Name?

These unique reptiles get their name from their ability to puff out a flap of skin under their chin when they feel threatened or show dominance, resembling a beard. This spiky "beard" can telegraph moods to other bearded dragons and indicate your beardie's health.

Wood Enclosures

Wood enclosures have many of the same advantages plastic enclosures have, such as front-facing glass doors, being lightweight, stackable, and having opaque sides. They also hold heat better, are more durable, and are less likely to break than glass enclosures. Some disadvantages to these enclosures include being harder to clean and sterilize and more easily damaged by moisture or water. However, if you are handy and love a good project, creating a custom-made wood enclosure is also an option. If needed, a quick internet search will give you creative ideas and instructions on how to make one.

Layout

A bearded dragon enclosure needs a hot side and a cooler side. The hot side is created by placing a heat lamp overhead. A light that provides UVB rays and bright white light for your dragon should be close to the heat lamp. A ceramic heat lamp is optional and only required if the temperature inside the enclosure drops too low.

At least one basking platform under the heat lamp and one hideaway on the cooler side should be in the enclosure. There should also be a shallow, nontoxic, BPA-free water and food dish. Additionally, there should be at least two thermometer gauges to monitor the hot and cool sides' temperatures and a hygrometer to measure and monitor the humidity levels. As a general rule, digital thermometers tend to be more accurate than analog thermometers.

A form of substrate should be on the bottom of the enclosure. Reptile carpet, tile, brown wrapping paper, indoor-outdoor carpet, newspaper, and paper towels are some of the most popular choices. If you choose a different option, ensure it won't cause health issues for your bearded dragon. Lastly, if your enclosure doesn't already have opaque sides, consider covering all three sides with a non-reflective backdrop like in the visual aid provided.

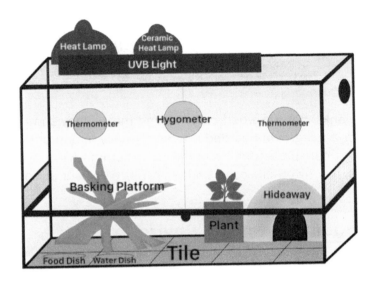

Furniture and Decorations

As you set up the enclosure for your bearded dragon, there are a few essential pieces of "furniture" your dragon needs. A platform is required to allow your bearded dragon to get close to its basking light. It can be an artificial rock, driftwood, or a commercial platform. A basking platform should never be electrically heated as they are notorious for causing burns.

Considering bearded dragons like to sleep, hide and brumate—a hibernation-like state for reptiles—a hideaway is essential to provide a secure and dark place for your dragon. Hideaways include plastic caves,

Photo Courtesy of Fraise Brady

wooden planks, natural wood caverns, and more. They should be big enough for a full-grown bearded dragon to move in and out of easily. Optional furniture pieces and decorations like hammocks, bridges, vines, and plants, among others, can be added to spice up your enclosure.

Creating a Naturalistic Environment

It's time to pull out your artistic side and have some fun creating a naturalistic environment in your enclosure, and it doesn't have to be extravagant. You can create a simple and visually appealing naturalistic environment by incorporating live or reptile-safe artificial plants, vines, flowers, a background, and a few natural pieces, like rocks, branches, and driftwood. I decided on artificial plants in my enclosure because I have what is known as a "brown thumb," and I didn't want to worry about the plants dying. I was surprised at how realistic they looked in my enclosure. I also chose artificial plants because I didn't want to worry about the enclosure's humidity levels rising. However, if you use live plants, ensure they are not toxic to your dragon. A short list of safe plants is aloe vera, turtle vine succulents, echeveria, haworthia, and prickly pear cactus with the spines removed. Safe herbs include rosemary, basil, oregano, and parsley.

Temperature and Lighting Requirements

> "
>
> *It's very important that new owners understand their heating and lighting. Heating bulbs will blow, so always have a spare, and be aware of the life span of the UV (ultraviolet) bulb. Just because a UV bulb is producing light does not mean it's still producing UV. Each UV bulb will have a recommendation from the manufacturer to change it after six, nine, or twelve months (usually). This needs to be done religiously, so mark in your calendar when you add the new bulb to the enclosure, and throw the old one out, even if it is still giving off light.*
>
> CHRISTY BRUCKNER
>
> *Reptile Cymru*
>
> "

Understanding the temperature and lighting requirements for a bearded dragon is usually the most challenging issue for beginners. All the new foreign terminology and countless heating and lighting options can be overwhelming. To summarize, you will have to mimic the sun in your enclosure through heat and light sources to supply your bearded dragon with three components it depends on for survival: UVA and UVB rays and heat.

Basking Area and Cool Area

The basking area is an especially hot spot in your enclosure where your dragon goes to warm

Photo Courtesy of Katie Stanley

up. The basking area needs to be 95°F to 110°F, depending on the age of your dragon. On the opposite side of the enclosure is the cooler side. The temperature for the cooler side needs to be 75 °F to 90°F, depending on your beardie's age. There should be a gradual decrease in temperature from the hot side to the cooler side, called a temperature gradient. The area between the hot and the cooler side should fall between the hot and cooler side's temperatures. The following are guidelines to provide your dragon with the correct temperatures for its age.

Age	Day Temperature	Night Temperature	Humidity
Baby	Basking Area: 100°F–110°F Cool Area: 80°F–90°F	70°F–75°F; No lower than 65°F	30%–40%
Juvenile	Basking Area: 95°F–100°F Cool Area: 75°F–80°F	70°F–75°F; No lower than 65°F	30%–40%
Adult	Basking Area: 95°F–100°F Cool Area: 75°F–80°F	70°F–75°F; No lower than 65°F	30%–40%

Heat Lamps and UVB Lights

When providing proper heating and lighting in your enclosure, the goal is to find the correct bulb or bulbs for your specific enclosure that give off the right amount of UVA, UVB, and heat. The lamps and lights used to achieve the goal can look different for each person. A contactless digital thermometer gun will significantly simplify setting your enclosure up by giving quick temperature readings for anywhere in your enclosure.

Heat Lamps

To metabolize and function, a bearded dragon's internal temperature needs to be between 95°F to 110°F. The best way for your beardie to reach its optimal temperature is by creating a basking area using an overhead heat source instead of sources like heat mats, rocks, or heat tape. Most light bulbs produce heat, except for fluorescent tubes and compact fluorescent bulbs, and come in various wattages and types. The higher the wattage, the more heat it emits.

The exact bulb wattage you will need primarily depends on your enclosure type and size. For reference purposes, a 100-watt bulb works well for a 40-gallon enclosure. All heat bulbs need an appropriate fixture that can withstand high heat, accommodate the bulb's wattage, and is designed for that specific bulb. Depending on your enclosure type, flexible light fixtures are a sensible choice as they allow you to adjust the distance of the light to your bearded dragon to find and maintain the correct temperature.

Photo Courtesy of Andi Smith

A baby bearded dragon needs a light and heat cycle of approximately 14 hours during the daytime and a 10-hour cycle with no heat or lights at night. Likewise, adult bearded dragons need about 12 hours of daytime heat and lighting, with no heat or lighting for 12 hours at night. To get a little more technical with your setup, replicate the day and night cycle to match your natural area. This could mean reducing the hours of lighting and heating during the fall and winter months and increasing them during the spring and summer seasons.

Household Incandescent

You can use any clear household incandescent light bulb in your enclosure for daytime heat and lighting. Look for a bulb labeled "daylight" and not "soft white." While incandescent bulbs are inexpensive, they are not as energy efficient, don't last as long, and don't give off light as widely as other bulbs.

Halogen Floodlights and Spotlights

Most hardware stores have a supply of halogen floodlights and spotlights. They make an excellent option for providing your dragon with a broad and moderately intense daytime basking area. Spotlight and

Photo Courtesy of Courtney Hart

floodlight bulbs are designed with a reflector built in, which causes most of the heat and light emitted to be pushed downward. They cost more and run hotter than a regular household incandescent light bulb of the same wattage but usually last twice as long.

Basking Bulbs

Heat bulbs specifically advertised for reptiles are sold under the name "basking bulbs." Basking bulbs provide the focused beam of heat and bright light needed in your enclosure, just like a regular incandescent or halogen bulb. They come in different bulb types, such as incandescent, mercury, and halogen. Other than being more expensive, there are minimal differences between reptile basking bulbs and regular incandescent and halogen bulbs.

Ceramic Heat Emitters

Ceramic heat emitters aren't required and aren't always necessary as long as your enclosure temperature doesn't dip below 65°F at night. However, they are the best option for supplementing heat sources at nighttime as they give off heat but don't emit visible light. They won't interfere with your bearded dragon's sleep cycle as infrared bulbs can. The wattage you'll want depends on how much of an increase in temperature is needed and the enclosure size.

UVB Lights

UVB lights are essential to any bearded dragon setup because they mimic the sun's UVB rays. UVB gives bearded dragons the ability to produce Vitamin D3, which aids calcium absorption. Without a UVB light, your dragon will develop metabolic bone disease, a painful, heartbreaking, and entirely preventable disease. Just as crucial to bearded dragons is UVA light. UVA rays are responsible for allowing your dragon to fight infection and stimulate and maintain its appetite and energy. Most UVB bulbs give off plenty of bright white light to supply your dragon with enough UVA rays.

The output of UVB is labeled on each bulb package as a percentage. Bearded dragons need a UVB output of at least 8% to 10%. Over time, UVB bulbs lose their strength; therefore, you will need to replace them within the time the manufacturer advises, even if they still appear to be working. All UVB basking lights should be operating at the same time as the heat lamp. Ideally, the light should span two-thirds to three-fourths of the enclosure. Three common types of UVB lights are mercury vapor bulbs, fluorescent linear tubes, and compact bulbs.

Mercury Vapor

Mercury vapor bulbs are an excellent option that simultaneously emits heat, UVA, and UVB rays. These bulbs last longer than fluorescent bulbs and use less energy but cost more to purchase. Use them with caution due to the high concentration levels of UVB. The first signs that your dragon is receiving too much UVB exposure are if it is closing or squinting its eyes when basking or has swollen eyes. Furthermore, ensure you give your dragon plenty of space to move in and out of the UVB rays.

Photo Courtesy of Cortney Farr

*Photo Courtesy of
Graham Fedrick*

Fluorescent Linear UVB Tubes

Fluorescent linear tubes designed for reptiles are another great option. They provide high-intensity UVB, light output, and excellent coverage at a lower cost. Of the countless UVB tubes available, two common types of linear tubes obtainable are called T5 tubes and T8 tubes. A T5 tube offers a higher output of UVB and brighter light than a T8 tube and is usually mounted outside an enclosure. T8 tubes are meant for smaller enclosures, and because they have lower UVB output, they need to be mounted inside the enclosure in most cases.

Compact/Coiled UVB Bulbs

Compact UVB bulbs have improved over the years, but not enough to come highly recommended. They have a limited range, don't last as long, and output fewer UVB rays than fluorescent tubes. They are a more suitable choice for reptiles and amphibians that require smaller amounts of UVB output and smaller enclosures. Since your enclosure will be big enough to fit a full-sized fluorescent tube, you should go that route instead.

Maintaining Correct Temperature Levels and Lighting

Thermostats and automatic timers are products you can use to maintain correct temperature levels and lighting in your enclosure. Thermostats are beneficial and, in my opinion, a must-have because they automatically monitor temperatures and prevent your enclosure from getting too hot or too cold. They automatically and subtly turn the heat lamp on or off to keep the enclosure within the preset temperature. Likewise, automatic timers are helpful because they turn lights and heat on or off at specific times and to a particular schedule to replicate a natural day and night cycle.

Monitoring Temperature and Light

Monitoring your enclosure's temperatures and lighting is easy and quick. You can monitor your enclosure's temperatures by reading the thermometers throughout the day. Overnight temperatures need to be checked periodically as well. Use a contactless digital thermometer gun for the most accurate and fastest reading anywhere in your enclosure. Don't forget to check the humidity level too. The best way to monitor the lights in your enclosure is to check your bulbs often to ensure they are working correctly and by keeping track of when to replace your UVB bulb as recommended by the manufacturer.

Photo Courtesy of Robert Brunning

Cleaning and Maintenance

> "
>
> *Daily spot cleaning of poops is something that really helps mainte-nance. Weekly soaks in a sink with a couple of inches of water and a light scrub with a toothbrush will keep your dragon hydrated and clean! Weekly and monthly deep cleans are good to keep your dragon's enclosure visually pleasant and keep your dragon happy and healthy. A good monthly maintenance would be to check your supplies just to make sure you have everything on hand.*
>
> MARK DOHMEN AND KATIE GROVE
>
> *Midwest Dragons*
>
> "

Being proactive and creating a cleaning routine is one of the best ways to maintain a hygienic enclosure. Typically, bearded dragons are odorless, relatively clean reptiles. The only time your bearded dragon gets messy and stinky is when it eliminates waste, which can happen mul-tiple times a day if it's a baby beardie. Keep the enclosure free of feces, dead bugs, and old food to reduce the bacteria that cause salmonella and to create an odorless enclosure.

Frequency and Method of Cleaning

Your bearded dragon's enclosure needs to be spot-cleaned daily and deep-cleaned monthly to keep it looking in tip-top shape and to keep your dragon healthy. Sometimes spot-cleaning needs to happen multiple times a day. It's essential to keep the enclosure as clean as possible to prevent spreading diseases. It will become a routine habit as you become familiar with what needs to be cleaned and how to clean it effectively.

Photo Courtesy of
Mikayla Sullivan

Deep Cleaning

It is necessary to deep-clean your enclosure once a month. For a deep clean, you first want to remove your bearded dragon from the enclosure and put it somewhere safe, like an empty bin or bathtub. I recommend wearing protective gloves during the cleaning process. After you put your gloves on, you should take these steps:

1. Remove all decorations, furniture, and substrate unless it's tile.
2. Spray the entire enclosure with disinfectant spray specially designed for reptiles, and follow the directions on the bottle. You can make your own solution by mixing half water and half vinegar and putting it in a spray bottle. There are many reptile recipes online to try. If you use the vinegar solution, you should let it sit for a minute or two to sanitize.
3. Wipe the enclosure dry with a paper towel.
4. Clean the decorations and furniture the same way you cleaned the inside of the enclosure, then rinse them off with water.
5. Replace the substrate.
6. Return the dry furniture and decorations to the enclosure.
7. Disinfect the surfaces with which the nonsterilized items came into contact, including the sink or tub you used for rinsing.
8. Depending on your protective gloves, don't forget to disinfect them or throw them away and wash your hands.

Photo Courtesy of Rene Mancourt

Maintaining the Habitat

Maintaining your dragon's habitat is quite simple, and once you do it a couple of times, it becomes second nature. Sometimes maintaining the habitat involves rolling up your sleeves, putting some gloves on, and cleaning up smelly things like poop. If your dragon has eliminated waste, you must remove it and clean the substrate. It's also crucial for you to promptly remove dead insects and uneaten food daily and wash the food and water bowls often.

Spotting and Addressing Common Issues

Being able to spot and address any issues your enclosure might encounter helps to maintain a hygienic enclosure and beardie. Two common issues that can occur are odors and pests. These issues need to be remedied by you promptly. Failure to address the issues straightaway can soon become a much larger problem.

Odor

If you have a foul odor coming from the enclosure, you need
to decipher if it's coming from the
enclosure or your beardie. If your
beardie is the reason for the foul
smell, it will require a bath. You
can find the proper way to bathe
your bearded dragon in Chapter
Five. If the odor is not from your
bearded dragon, check the entire
enclosure for any uneaten food,
dead insects, or feces and remove
them. If there is no waste, uneaten
food, or dead insects, and the
odor lingers, you need to deep-
clean your enclosure.

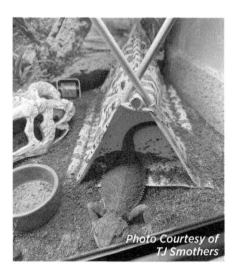

*Photo Courtesy of
TJ Smothers*

Pests

Small black flying insects in your enclosure, like houseflies or fruit
flies, can be problematic. Although they are small, they can cause significant problems for your dragon. They can be hard for you to get rid
of and, if eaten, can give your dragon parasites and harmful bacteria.
They frequently hitchhike their way into your enclosure on fresh fruits
or vegetables and are attracted to the sweet smell of decaying food. To
eliminate these pests, remove all uneaten fruit or vegetables and clean
the enclosure and everything in it, including replacing the substrate. As
I mentioned above, they can be hard to get rid of; therefore, I recommend placing a fruit fly or fly trap near the enclosure but not within reach
of your dragon.

CHAPTER 3

Nutrition and Diet

> **"**
>
> *A varied diet is good for your dragon's health, both mental and physical. Try adding new things now and then and giving treats to keep it stimulated and healthy. Calcium and multivitamins are crucial and should not be skipped for any reason.*
>
> CHRISTY BRUCKNER
>
> *Reptile Cymru*
>
> **"**

Bearded dragons live and breathe for their simple life of basking, bugs, and leafy greens. Like all exotic animals, dragons' nutritional needs require more care and attention than the average pet. Their diet is flexible, but there are some guidelines to follow. By fulfilling your bearded dragon's nutritional and dietary requirements, your pet will be healthier and have greater longevity.

Diet in the Wild

> *Variety is the spice of life. Just like humans, animals tend to get bored with the same nutritional diet, so you have to vary their diet as they grow. For the first year of their life, there's an 80–20 rule; you should have 80% of their diet be insects and 20% should be greens. As they get older, it reverts, and you can do 20% insects and 80% greens, making sure you always supplement with calcium.*
>
> FRANCISCO E. AQUINO SANCHEZ
> *Rhegal Dragons*

Out in the wild, bearded dragons are omnivorous reptiles that eat both insects and plants. The term "omnivore" comes from the Latin words omni, meaning "all, everything," and vovare, translating to "to devour or swallow." They will devour almost everything they encounter. Since they often experience hunger during times of famine in Australia, they can't afford to be picky eaters, and they are not.

Types of Insects, Plants, and Other Foods

Bearded dragons are ravenous lizards, feeding greedily on nearly any insect in the wild that moves. With their sharp vision and keen sense of smell, they find termites, ants, beetles, grubs, crickets, cockroaches, and worms to gorge upon. They will also consume leaves, weeds, flowers, and some fruits. Additionally, it's not uncommon for bearded dragons to occasionally eat a mouse or small lizard—even a lizard of their own species.

Natural Feeding Behavior and Habits

Bearded dragons are ferocious and opportunistic hunters in Australia's most hostile and unforgiving terrain. They seize every opportunity to ingest enough insects, small vertebrates, or vegetation to satisfy their enormous appetites. These lizards can go without water for days and receive much of the hydration they need from their food. Despite food and water being scarce at times in their environment, their ability to thrive is credited to their resourceful foraging and aggressive hunting skills. When they aren't actively searching for food, they often strategically place themselves at an elevated level, lie still, and wait for the opportunity to leap on top of unsuspecting prey.

Nutritional Requirements

Bearded dragons require a specialized diet to meet their nutritional needs. They need macronutrients from carbs, proteins, and fats, micronutrients found in vitamins and minerals, and adequate water. The only way to meet these nutritional requirements is by providing the appropriate foods for your lizard. The foods they need will evolve as they mature from baby bearded dragons—requiring a diet primarily of insects—to adult dragons—mainly consuming vegetables.

Mimicking the Natural Diet in Captivity

66

Feed your dragon a good variety of food, including veggies, greens, fruits, and insects. Getting your dragon established with Repashy gelatin formulas is a great way to keep your pet hydrated, and it is packed with lots of insect protein and vegetables. Dusting your dragon's food with calcium powder will aid in preventing MBD (metabolic bone disease). We also spray our dragons a few times daily with water, as they love to drink off their faces.

MARK DOHMEN AND KATIE GROVE

Midwest Dragons

99

One of the best things you can provide your bearded dragon with in captivity is a diet that mimics its natural one as closely as possible. Feed your dragon a varied and balanced diet consisting of live insects, raw vegetables, and some fruit. Remember, variety is crucial; your beardie should not be given the same foods repetitively.

HEALTH ALERT
Eat Your Greens

Bearded dragons thrive on a varied diet of vegetation and insects. Therefore, a well-rounded diet for these reptiles should include leafy greens, fruits, flowers, crickets, and worms. A varied diet is essential to ensure that your pet's nutritional needs are met and can even provide some necessary mental stimulation for your reptile. In addition to an intriguing game of chase, live insects offer crucial nutrients to your bearded dragon, including phosphorus, iron, vitamin A, and calcium.

Feeder Insects

Most experts agree that feeding your dragon live insects is the best way to provide it with protein and other required nutrients. Live insects also benefit your lizard by providing mental stimulation and activating natural feeding behaviors. Most pet stores carry the insects your bearded dragon will require. You can also purchase live insects online from companies that conveniently deliver them to your front door.

Feeder insects come in all sorts of sizes. Some insects are as small as a pinhead, and others can reach several inches long. A bearded dragon can choke on insects that are too large or may not effectively digest them. Therefore, the length of the insect shouldn't exceed the width between your bearded dragon's eyes. Some insects are also toxic, risk being contaminated with chemicals, or can pass parasites on to your bearded dragon. Avoid feeding your beardie:

- Insects found outside
- Insects sold for fishing at bait shops or stores
- Insects found inside your home
- Dead insects
- Any insects that glow, including fireflies/lightning bugs
- Elderbugs

Staple Feeder Insects

> **"**
>
> *Crickets keep your bearded dragon both active and hydrated. Provided they come from a quality source, they are the most underrated feeder.*
>
> BLAKE MCNEELY
> *Cliffhanger Reptiles*
> **"**

A "staple" feeder is an insect that meets the nutritional needs of your beardie with no adverse side effects when consumed daily. The most popular and widely accessible staples are Dubia roaches and crickets. Additional staple insects that may be harder to find in pet stores include red runner roaches, discoid roaches, orange head roaches, Turkestan roaches, silkworms, black fly larvae, and many more. It's worth mentioning that Dubia roaches are illegal to own or import to places like Florida, Hawaii, and Canada. So, be sure to check the laws in your area and find an alternative insect if you live in a place that prohibits them.

Non-Staple Feeder Insects

Some live feeder insects, like hornworms, goliath worms, superworms, waxworms, earthworms, and mealworms, are not considered a staple for your pet. They fail to provide a balanced range of nutrients and can cause dietary imbalances or deficiencies if fed daily to your lizard. These feeder insects can make up a part of your bearded dragon's varied diet when occasionally used to supplement other insects. Although you can periodically feed waxworms and butterworms to young bearded dragons, you should only feed them to adult bearded dragons as a treat due to their high-fat content.

Dubai Roaches

Storing and Caring for Feeder Insects

Storing and caring for your feeder insects is not complicated. All insects should be kept in a well-ventilated storage container. For most insects, the container they come in usually works fine. However, crickets can quickly jump out of small containers and need a cricket keeper found at pet stores or a deep plastic tote. Additionally, plastic tote lids will need ventilation added. All feeder insects should be stored in a dry, dark place, away from direct sunlight. The temperature they need to be kept at will vary by the insect, with some needing refrigeration. Since the care instructions for feeder insects differ from insect to insect, ask the store or breeder about the specific care they will need.

Gut-Loading Feeder Insects

Gut-loading feeder insects is an excellent way to maximize their nutritional value, which then, in turn, is passed on to your bearded dragon. You can gut-load your feeder insects by offering them plant-based foods to eat for about 24 hours before you feed them to your bearded dragon. The food you give your feeder insects should be food that won't cause harm to your bearded dragon. Some suitable foods are commercial gut-loading products, carrots, leafy greens, whole-grain bread, oats, potatoes, apples, and squash.

Preparing Feeder Insects

Lightly dust all feeder insects, except black fly larvae, with a quality calcium powder before feeding them to your bearded dragon. Dusting insects prevents calcium deficiencies that can lead to numerous health issues. Additionally, insects also need to be dusted with a multivitamin powder. How often owners need to dust insects is controversial within the bearded dragon community. Netherlands bearded dragon breeder Renzo, from OlympicBeardedDragon, recommends giving *"calcium without Vitamin D3 every day as a supplement and vitamins once every two weeks, but don't give calcium powder on the day vitamins are given."* If you have any doubts about how often to dust your insects, consult with a veterinarian.

How to Dust Feeder Insects

Cricket shakers, 32-ounce deli cups, and resealable plastic sandwich bags make dusting feeder insects quick and easy. A word of advice: winged insects are hard for bearded dragons to digest and, in fact, often come out whole. Therefore, I recommend breaking their wings off before dusting them with powder. The following is an example of how to dust feeder insects with powder in a resealable plastic bag.

1. Place a small pinch or two of powder into the bag.
2. Put enough insects for one feeding inside the bag.
3. Leave air in the bag and seal it closed.
4. Hold the top of the bag tightly with your hand and gently shake the bag to cover the insects in powder.
5. Feed the dusted insects to your bearded dragon without delay.

Serving Feeder Insects

There are a couple of ways to feed insects to your bearded dragon. One way is to offer your bearded dragon insects individually using small tweezers or tongs found at pet stores. If the feeder insects are worms, another option is to put them on top of your beardie's daily salad. Another alternative is to put your bearded dragon and the insects together in a different enclosure or container and let it chase after the insects. You can also put the feeder insects into a smaller container and let your bearded dragon eat out of it. To make feeding crickets to your bearded dragon easier, slow the insects down by putting them into a sealable plastic bag and then into a refrigerator for five minutes.

Avoid feeding insects in the same enclosure your bearded dragon inhabits to prevent complications and make cleaning up after the meal easy. Complications can occur when feeder insects, primarily crickets, escape and hide underneath the substrate or inside and underneath decorations. Crickets can be especially hazardous as they are known to bite bearded dragons when they are sleeping, inflicting injuries and causing stress. Feeding your bearded dragon in a separate location, such as a plastic tub or spare enclosure, will also allow you to closely monitor how much your dragon is eating.

Photo Courtesy of Nicole Rowe

Vegetables and Fruits

Photo Courtesy of Theresa A. Bedno

Regardless of its age, your bearded dragon needs vegetables daily, specifically dark leafy green ones, alongside insects. The best leafy green vegetables are nutrient-dense, low in oxalates, phosphorus, and goitrogens, and high in calcium. A diet high in oxalates and phosphorus prevents calcium absorption in bearded dragons' bodies, which can lead to significant health issues. Likewise, a diet too high in goitrogens will induce thyroid issues in your lizard. Since fruits are generally mineral-poor, they should be given to your bearded dragon sparingly.

Benefits of a Diet of Vegetables and Fruit

A diet rich in vegetables and fruits adds water to your bearded dragon's body to help keep it hydrated. It also helps prevent deficiencies that negatively impact your pet's look, energy level, mood, and overall quality of life.

Incorporating Vegetables and Fruits into Your Beardie's Diet

Rotating vegetables and a few fruits throughout the month is a great way to keep your beardie's diet balanced and varied. Without a balanced diet, your pet will be susceptible to diseases, sicknesses, and fatigue. In addition, switching up the foods you serve to your bearded dragon keeps things interesting, thereby increasing its appetite.

Safe and Nutritional Fruits and Vegetables

Like staple and non-staple insects, your bearded dragon can con-sume staple vegetables daily and eat non-staple vegetables throughout the month in rotation. Not all foods are safe for your bearded dragon.

	Daily Staple	On Rotation Throughout the Month	Avoid
Greens	Endive Mustard Greens Turnip Greens Collard Greens Dandelion Greens	Basil Parsley Parsnip Carrot Tops Bok Choy Cilantro Radicchio	Romaine Lettuce Iceberg Lettuce Tomato Leaves Spinach
Vegetables	Yellow Squash Acorn Squash Butternut Squash Spaghetti Squash	Bell Peppers Carrots Artichoke Hearts Asparagus Cucumbers Pumpkins Peas Yams Zucchini Carrots Celery	Leeks Rhubarb Chives Garlic Mushrooms Onions Hot Peppers Edamame
Fruit	Prickly Pear	Apricots Bananas Blackberries Kiwi Raspberries Mango Blueberries Grapes Peaches Strawberries Pears	Avocados Oranges Grapefruit Pineapple Lemons Limes

Preparing Vegetables and Fruits

To prepare fresh vegetables and fruits for your beardie, always thoroughly wash them with water first to remove physical contaminants and germs. Raw fruits and vegetables contain the most nutrients and make the best choice to give to your bearded dragon. However, if the vegetable is too hard, like pumpkin and squash, boil or steam it long enough to soften it. You can also use a cheese grater to shred it into small pieces instead of cooking it. Do not give any vegetable pieces to your bearded dragon that are too hard or that haven't cooled to room temperature. Furthermore, bearded dragons should not eat any vegetable or fruit seeds.

The most convenient way to serve vegetables to your bearded dragon is to create a small salad. Premixed salad bags commonly found in the produce department in stores, like spring mixes, make a convenient base

*Photo Courtesy of
Alyssa Vargas*

for the salad. Avoid feeding spinach-based mixes, which aren't safe for your lizard, as spinach is high in oxalates. Additionally, avoid lettuces like iceberg and romaine, as lettuce contains minimal nutrients. If you use leafy green vegetables that come in a bunch, cut them into small pieces or strips to create your salad base. For all other vegetables and fruits, finely chop them into small pieces to be mixed into or put on top of the salad greens.

Water

Water is essential to your bearded dragon's diet. A dehydrated bearded dragon can suffer many health problems, such as constipation, kidney failure, and gout. Therefore, supply your bearded dragon every day with clean water to drink. If you are using tap water, treat it with a reptile-specific water conditioner that removes chloramines and chlorine. You can also purchase filtered or bottled water instead. Since not all bearded dragons will drink from a dish, it is beneficial to lightly sprinkle water on the salad or your bearded dragon's head.

Commercially Prepared Bearded Dragon Food

Commercially prepared foods for bearded dragons found online or in pet stores are a good way to add variety to your bearded dragon's diet. Since they are ready-to-eat, easy to use, and specially formulated with premium plant and animal ingredients with added vitamins and minerals, they offer a great source of nutrients for your reptile. Additionally, commercial food is excellent to have as a backup when needed. Even though commercially prepared foods help create variety in your beardie's diet and are convenient to have on hand, they should be given in addition to and not as a substitute for live insects, fresh vegetables, and fruit.

Photo Courtesy of
Colette Steinhauer

Types of Commercially Prepared Bearded Dragon Food

The most popular commercially prepared beardie food comes in the form of pellets. Additional commercial food options include bites, canned, gel premixes, and dried food. Commercially prepared foods that contain insects, like freeze-dried and canned options, work great as a topping alongside chopped vegetables in your bearded dragon's salad.

Pros and Cons of Commercially Prepared Food

From their ability to be stored easily to the very little preparation they require, there is no denying that commercial foods are super convenient. However, commercial foods are not as healthy as a raw and natural diet and won't stimulate your bearded dragon mentally since it won't have to hunt for this type of food. Furthermore, this kind of food is costlier. Lastly, not all bearded dragons take to commercially prepared food, with some even rejecting it altogether.

Choosing a High-Quality Commercial Food

To choose a high-quality commercial food, carefully read the nutritional labels and package information to select a nutrient-dense and balanced brand appropriate for your bearded dragon's age. The best commercial foods are made from all-natural ingredients with no artificial colors, flavors, or preservatives. If you are unsure about which commercial food is best for your bearded dragon, be sure to consult with a veterinarian.

Feeding Schedule and Portion Sizes

As you establish a feeding schedule with your bearded dragon, it will begin to anticipate its feeding times. A schedule will also help you to remember to feed your bearded dragon daily. Furthermore, providing your lizard with the correct portion sizes will help keep it at a healthy weight.

Photo Courtesy of Danielle Spradlin

Determining Appropriate Portion Size and Feeding Schedule

To determine the amount of food your bearded dragon needs, you will need to consider your bearded dragon's age, size, and activity level. Since your captive bearded dragon isn't as active as its wild counterparts, it will not need to consume nearly as much food as they do. However, active bearded dragons will still need more food than sedentary dragons.

After the basking light turns on in the morning, your bearded dragon will warm up underneath it for 20 minutes or more. Some bearded dragons are ready to eat their first meal after 20 minutes, while others need more time basking. Most bearded dragons will fill up on insects if given a chance. Therefore, offering your bearded dragon its salad first is a good idea, allowing some time to pass before offering insects. When feeding your bearded dragon in the evening, do it at a time that will allow at least two hours of basking after your beardie eats its dinner in order to ensure proper digestion.

How Often and How Much to Feed a Bearded Dragon

Your bearded dragon needs a fresh salad daily, regardless of age, even if it doesn't eat it each time. A baby bearded dragon will greatly benefit from being offered a salad daily, as it is a great way to familiarize the lizard with the food it will eat most as an adult. Offer half a cup of salad for babies, three-fourths of a cup for juveniles, and one and a half cups for adults daily. Incorporate all other fruits and vegetables into your beardie's diet in small amounts. Salads can remain in the enclosure all day or until they show signs of wilting.

Expect to feed your bearded dragon as many insects as it can consume in a 10-to-15-minute period. Remove any uneaten insects after each feeding session. A baby bearded dragon needs four to five feedings daily. Juveniles need three to four feedings daily, and sub-adult bearded dragons need feedings twice daily. As your bearded dragon matures into an adult, it will need one feeding daily. As a point of reference, baby and juvenile bearded dragons can consume roughly 25 to 50 roaches in one day, and adults can eat approximately three to five roaches a day.

Life Stage	Ratio	Frequency (Times Per Day)
Baby	20% Insects 80% Vegetables	4–5
Juvenile (4–12 Months)	70% Insects 30% Vegetables	3
Sub Adult (12–18 Months)	30% Insects 70% Vegetables	2
Adult (18 Months+)	20% Insects 80% Vegetables	1

Photo Courtesy of
Elizabeth Weedall

Monitoring Weight and Adjusting Feeding
Schedule Accordingly

The simplest and most accurate way to monitor your bearded dragon's weight is by using a small scale. Some people use mechanical kitchen scales to weigh their dragons, but compact digital scales with a large range in grams are most accurate. However, if you don't have a scale, there are physical signs to look for that indicate if your bearded dragon is under or overweight.

An obese lizard can suffer from many health issues that can shorten its life expectancy. If your dragon regularly has a large belly that drags on the ground, ribs you can't feel, and bulging fat pads behind its eyes, abdomen, and on the base of its tail, this indicates that your bearded dragon is overweight. Cut back on food slowly, offer more vegetables and fewer insects, and encourage your dragon to be more active.

An underweight bearded dragon has even more significant potential for serious health issues than an overweight one. Signs your bearded dragon is underweight include protruding hip bones, a thin tail, and deflated fat pads on the body. If your bearded dragon appears to be skinny, slowly add more fat to its diet and increase the number of feeding sessions until a healthy weight is reached. Some foods higher in fat include mealworms, waxworms, and superworms. If feeding your bearded dragon foods higher in fat doesn't resolve the problem, schedule an appointment with a veterinarian to rule out any underlying health issues. You can use the following table to reference what is within a healthy weight range for your bearded dragon.

Age (Months)	Weight (Grams)
0–1	4–6
1–2	8–40
2–3	22–110
3–4	41–115
4–5	102–115
5–6	183–188
6–7	230–288
7–8	252–327
9–10	280–360
11–12	350–465
12+	380–500

CHAPTER 4

Handling and Training

> "
>
> *Most bearded dragons get used to being touched, but excessive handling can cause stress. Especially if you've just gotten your bearded dragon, it's best to let it get used to its new home first. When you do handle the dragon, support the entire body from below, especially the front and hind legs. Squeezing or gripping too tightly is not a good idea. In general, don't take your bearded dragon out of the terrarium for more than fifteen minutes; even though it may sit sweetly with you, the cold will cause the dragon to go into a resting state.*
>
> RENZO
>
> *OlympicBeardedDragon*
>
> "

One of the extraordinary qualities that attract people to bearded dragons in the first place is how easy they are to handle. There is just something oh-so-special about holding a bearded dragon's perfect-sized body and feeling its unique texture under your fingers as it lies calmly in your hand. It is through regular handling that your bearded dragon will become comfortable being held by you, allowing a bond to form.

Photo Courtesy of
Graham Fedrick

How to Handle Your Bearded Dragon Safely and Gently

"

Wash your hands before and after handling. Be aware of the ambient temperature of the room you're letting the dragon into. If letting it outside, only do so supervised, being extremely aware of temperatures and of potential predators or places where the dragon can escape. Beardies can run surprisingly fast, so don't turn your back! If letting your pet wander around the living room, always supervise it and make sure the floor is clean and tidy. A customer of mine spent a lot of money on surgery to remove a coin that his dragon had swallowed while wandering around the room!

CHRISTY BRUCKNER

Reptile Cymru

"

Photo Courtesy of Christina Grace

Handling bearded dragons is usually an easy task because of their calm and laid-back personalities, but a bearded dragon not used to being held can feel threatened. Properly handling your beardie is necessary to prevent injury and needless stress. Learning to pick up, hold, and handle your pet correctly will also reduce your risk of getting scratched or bitten. Since most animals respond positively to routine, with proper and consistent handling, your bearded dragon will enjoy your company and look forward to engaging with you.

Proper Techniques for Handling a Bearded Dragon

Before you handle your beardie, make sure it's during a quiet and calm time and in a controlled setting. If your bearded dragon is untamed, it can take longer for the lizard to get used to you and your interactions. In general, keep handling sessions short, between five to 15 minutes, especially at first, to keep your bearded dragon's stress levels low. To properly handle your dragon:

1. Wash your hands before you handle your bearded dragon.
2. As you approach your dragon in its enclosure, make your presence known from a distance to avoid startling it.
3. Slowly open the enclosure door and move one hand toward your bearded dragon, keeping your hand in its front line of sight. Watch for signs of aggression or distress like darkening of the beard, hissing, or attempting to bite. If you don't observe these behaviors,

proceed to the next step. If you see signs of distress or aggression, slowly pull your hand away from your dragon and try again later.

4. Gently pet and softly talk to your bearded dragon to get it accustomed to your hand and voice.

5. Move your hand slowly, with palm upturned, under your bearded dragon's body and gently scoop it up, supporting its entire body from underneath. Gently put your other hand on top of your lizard or under its tail for extra support.

6. When the handling session ends, gently return your bearded dragon to its enclosure.

7. Make sure you wash your hands after handling your bearded dragon.

Avoiding Common Handling Mistakes

Bearded dragons don't like being taken by surprise and will respond better to handling when they expect it. Therefore, avoid sneaking up on your pet. Additionally, when you handle your bearded dragon, never grab it by its tail, limbs, or neck or lay it on its back. You should also never forcefully restrain or squeeze your beardie at any time. Furthermore, avoid handling your bearded dragon while other pets are around or after it has just eaten food. Lastly, prevent your bearded dragon from getting injured by handling it from a lower elevation, especially if it's a baby beardie that is more likely to jump off your hand.

HELPFUL TIP
The Ideal Roommate

Like humans, bearded dragons are diurnal, meaning they are most active during the day and sleep at night. Being aware of your bearded dragon's sleep schedule can help you get the most out of your bonding time by limiting your bonding activities to the hours when your reptile is most active. For example, establishing a consistent routine that aligns with your bearded dragon's optimal sleeping schedule will help eliminate potential stressors for your pet and create a positive cohabitation environment. Most bearded dragons enjoy eight to 12 hours of sleep per night in captivity, slightly more than the average human.

Bonding with Your Bearded Dragon

> ❝
> *Always make sure to support the front and back legs when handling a bearded dragon. Younger dragons can be flighty and run away or jump, so hold on, but not too tight. As dragons grow, so does their confidence, and the running away and jumping will happen less. When dragons are small, they think everything wants to eat them. Over time your dragon will develop trust with you and become the best couch buddy!*
>
> MARK DOHMEN AND KATIE GROVE
> *Midwest Dragons*
> ❞

You can strengthen your bond with your bearded dragon through the experiences, attention, and care you provide. As with any relationship, it will take effort, commitment, and patience, but in no time, you and your bearded dragon will be like two peas in a pod.

Regular Handling and Interaction

Photo Courtesy of Erika Rivera

The more time you spend handling and interacting with your bearded dragon, the more acquainted with each other you will become. When spending time with your dragon, gently talk to it and show affection by softly rubbing it underneath its chin, for example. Once your bearded dragon feels safe with you, you can participate in fun bonding activities. Some activities to bond over include baths, watching television, taking walks, swimming, exploring the house, spending time outdoors, and playing with cat toys.

Providing a Suitable Environment and Diet

Let your bearded dragon know that you care about its well-being and health by providing the best diet and enclosure setup possible. Be committed to providing an enclosure that closely resembles its habitat in the wild, and rearrange the contents occasionally to keep your bearded dragon from getting bored. Provide the nutrient-dense and varied diet discussed in Chapter 3. Periodically hand-feed your bearded dragon to strengthen the bond between the two of you.

Understanding Your Bearded Dragon's Body Language

Understanding your bearded dragon's body language is also a great way to deepen the bond with your bearded dragon. For example, when you recognize behaviors that indicate your bearded dragon is unhappy, such as beard flaring and puffing up, you'll know to comfort and calm it down with gentle petting and talking. Appropriately responding to your bearded dragon's emotions will allow you and your pet to form a close attachment.

FUN FACT
How Popular Are They?

Due to their docile nature and manageable size, bearded dragons are currently one of the most popular pet lizards. Of the eight bearded dragon species, the most popular pet is the central bearded dragon or *Pogona vitticeps.*

Responding to Their Needs and Preferences

You can develop a strong bond with your bearded dragon by responding to its needs and preferences. Since your bearded dragon cannot meet its own needs in captivity, it will depend on you to provide those things for it, or it simply can't survive. You can strengthen your bond with your bearded dragon by paying close attention to nonverbal cues and body language that strongly convey what your dragon prefers or dislikes. For instance, our bearded dragon makes it clear which foods he enjoys most in his salads by eyeing them, eating them first, and then scavenging through the salad to make sure he hasn't missed any.

Training Your Bearded Dragon to Come When Called

Training your bearded dragon is a great way to spend quality time together and stimulate your bearded dragon's mind. It may come as a complete shock to you that your bearded dragon is intelligent enough to be taught to come to you when you call its name. Teaching your dragon any command can only happen after establishing a close bond. Training your beardie to follow this command is beneficial for its safety, as you can call your beardie out of hiding when it suddenly vanishes out of sight—which can happen in the blink of an eye.

Using Treats or Other Rewards

Since most bearded dragons are food-motivated, you can use insects or the food your dragon loves most during training sessions as motivation and a reward. Using the right food or insects is the difference between a highly motivated and focused dragon and an uninterested or distracted one. Treats will make training much more enjoyable for you and your bearded dragon.

Training Sessions

Training sessions should be short and consistent, keeping your bearded dragon engaged and focused. Be consistent but flexible by implementing a training session at least once a day. Patience and repetition are critical at each training session. Remember that your bearded dragon will not be able to learn commands overnight; it can take weeks or months. You will know your bearded dragon has mastered the command when it persistently comes to you without using a treat. To begin:

Photo Courtesy of Sha Davis

1. Say your bearded dragon's name and immediately give it a treat. You can do this step with your bearded dragon in or out of its enclosure.
2. Repeat the process for a few weeks.
3. After a week or more, move the training session to a safe location on the floor with your beardie close in front.
4. Say your dragon's name as you put the treat out in front of you to lure your pet toward you and give it a treat as a reward once it has reached you.
5. Repeat step 4 for two weeks, at least once a day.
6. Once your bearded dragon consistently comes to you from a short distance when called, increase the distance between you and the lizard slowly over time.

Photo Courtesy of Morgan Moons

Troubleshooting Common Problems and Challenges

Two common challenges owners face while training their bearded dragons is that they are not interested in the treats used during training sessions or aren't catching on. If your bearded dragon isn't catching on as quickly as you hoped, you may need to adjust your expectations. Since every bearded dragon differs, some will catch on quickly, while others may need more time. Remember to be patient and use this as a bonding opportunity.

Photo Courtesy of Katie Childress

If your dragon is not interested in the treat you use during training sessions, check if you are conducting training sessions when your pet is most hungry, like at regular mealtimes. Also, make sure the food you use as a treat is of high value to your lizard. The treat you use should make your beardie want to work for it. You may have to experiment with different food items or insects until you find one that interests and excites your bearded dragon.

CHAPTER 5

Health and Common Medical Issues

The leading causes of sickness amongst bearded dragons are vitamin and mineral deficiencies, stress, inadequate care, and failure to properly maintain the conditions of the enclosure. When their living conditions and diet are correct and they receive proper care, bearded dragons rarely get sick. When a bearded dragon does not behave as it usually does, it indicates something may be wrong. During times of uncertainty, taking your bearded dragon to a veterinarian with reptile experience is always recommended.

Photo Courtesy of Nicole Rowe

Basic Health Care and Grooming

Providing basic health care, like routine check-ups, parasite control, and preventative care, will positively impact and maximize your bearded dragon's quality of life. Another way to keep your pet healthy is through regular grooming. Cleaning its eyes and nose, trimming its claws, and giving it baths are vital to the well-being of your bearded dragon.

Cleaning Eyes and Nostrils

During shedding, it's common for a bearded dragon's nose to have a small piece of shed stuck in each nostril and around the eyes. Shed left in the nose is especially important to remove as breathing issues can occur. If your bearded dragon has stuck shed around its eyes, you can help free the shed by gently placing a cotton ball soaked in warm water on one eye at a time for several minutes. Gently use a pair of tweezers to remove stuck shed in the nostrils.

Trimming Nails

Your bearded dragon will need its nails cut every few weeks to prevent scratches and its nails from getting caught on things and being damaged. Overgrown nails can also force your bearded dragon's toes to twist. A bearded dragon with twisted toes will have difficulty gaining traction and climbing, and it will also cause discomfort. Trimming your bearded dragon's nails is easy and can be done using any nail clippers

DID YOU KNOW?
Basking

Bearded dragons are ectotherms, meaning they don't produce any of their own body heat. Therefore, these reptiles have a unique method of thermoregulation: basking. This behavior includes lying or "basking" under a heat source to raise their body temperature or moving to a cooler area to regulate it. The ideal temperature for a basking spot should be between 95 and 105 degrees Fahrenheit, with baby bearded dragons requiring slightly higher temps. Adequate heating is critical to bearded dragon digestion—without a heat source, your bearded dragon can't digest food.

Photo Courtesy of Adreannae Griggs

you already have. Just make sure you sanitize the nail clippers with rubbing alcohol before and after you use them. To trim your lizard's nails, cut a minuscule amount off the tip of the nail with your clippers. A veterinarian can do it if you are uncomfortable with cutting your pet's claws.

Bathing

Your bearded dragon will need to be bathed and soaked in water regularly. Regular baths will keep your pet's body clean and hydrated, alleviate constipation, and aid with the shedding process. Bathing can take place in a bathtub, sink, or container. If you are giving your bearded dragon a bath in the bathtub or sink, rinse the tub of any shampoo, conditioner, or soap residue beforehand. When helping your dragon with shedding, allow your beardie to soak for an additional 15 to 20 minutes during the bathing process. Soak your dragon in water one to three times a week and give it a quick bath when necessary. To bathe your bearded dragon:

1. Fill the container, sink, or tub with warm water no higher than your bearded dragon's knees. Don't add any soaps or cleaners to the water. The ideal water temperature is around 85 to 95°F.
2. Put your bearded dragon into the tub, sink, or container. You should be present and monitor your dragon for the entire bath.
3. Use a soft-bristle toothbrush to scrub your bearded dragon's body lightly. Avoid scrubbing your dragon's eyes, nose, or cloaca (end of the digestive tract).
4. When your bearded dragon is clean, take it out of the water to dry.
5. Dry your bearded dragon by gently patting it with a towel.
6. Return your dragon to its enclosure.
7. Sanitize the tub, sink, or container with a sanitizing solution.

Monitoring Health and Appearance

Closely monitor the health and appearance of your bearded dragon every day. Becoming familiar with what is typical for your bearded dragon and its general appearance is the only way you will be able to notice anything out of the ordinary. If you see any change in activity level, appetite, behavior, appearance, or feces, monitor it closely. Sometimes changes in behaviors or symptoms can return to normal by the end of the day, but if behaviors or symptoms persist or worsen, it's time to visit a veterinarian.

HEALTH ALERT
Tail Rot

Tail rot is a serious condition afflicting bearded dragons, resulting in rapid cell death in the beardie's tail. Several factors, including trauma, poor nutrition, or inadequate hygiene, can cause this disease. Signs of tail rot include tail color changes, dry tail scales, deformity, and, eventually, tail loss. Prompt treatment is critical for beardies with tail rot because failure to treat it can result in the complete loss of your lizard's tail. Unfortunately, unlike other lizards, bearded dragons can't regrow a tail that has fallen off.

Photo Courtesy of Stephanie Rarick

Identifying Potential Health Issues

Abnormal or atypical behaviors can signal that your bearded dragon has an underlying health issue. Early intervention is essential, and anything you believe to be abnormal or not typical for your bearded dragon should be thoroughly investigated by a reptile veterinarian. Signs or symptoms that signal a potential health issue include the following:

- Losing weight
- Lethargic
- Loss of appetite
- Wheezing, gasping, or coughing
- Puffy, bulging, or swollen eyes
- Eyes, nose, or mouth secretions
- Diarrhea, constipation, or bloody feces

- Skin changes
- Behavior changes
- Shaking, dizziness, head tilting

Common Health Issues and How to Prevent Them

> *Find a veterinary reptile specialist and have yearly check-ups to make sure your bearded dragon is clear of parasites. Then just always do a regular visual check of your bearded dragon. If you are vigilant about its demeanor, attitude, and daily activity you will be able to pick up on the subtle things that the dragon will be able to tell you, and you'll know if your bearded dragon is sick or not.*
>
> FRANCISCO E. AQUINO SANCHEZ
> *Rhegal Dragons*

Educating yourself on your bearded dragon's health and proactively managing it is essential. Taking the necessary proactive measures to prevent health issues starts from the moment you bring your new pet home. With all illnesses, the quicker they are detected and treated, the better the prognosis and the less likely there will be any long-term side effects. Many health issues seen in bearded dragons come on slowly and, therefore, can be challenging to detect at their earlier stages, which is why preventing them is so crucial.

Respiratory Infections

Upper respiratory infections, commonly called URIs, can be caused by bacteria, viruses, or fungi. URIs affect the lungs and breathing of a bearded dragon. The most common reasons they occur are improper enclosure temperatures and humidity. If you suspect your bearded dragon has a URI, make an appointment to be seen by a veterinarian as soon as possible. Here are some symptoms of a URI:

- Gaping
- Noisy breathing
- Gasping
- Slimy mucus-like discharge excreting from the mouth or nose
- Puffiness around the throat pouch

Parasites

Bearded dragons can easily get intestinal parasites by eating insects that host them. Even pet store insects can have parasites. If you think your dragon may have parasites, a trip to the vet will be necessary to determine the best medication. Symptoms due to intestinal parasites include the following:

- Profuse diarrhea
- Abnormal stool
- Particularly stinky feces
- Weakness
- Vomiting
- Lack of appetite
- Weight loss
- Lethargy

Photo Courtesy of Theresa A. Bedno

Metabolic Bone Disease

Metabolic bone disease (MBD) is a severe and life-threatening but entirely preventable disease that is all too common in bearded dragons. MBD occurs when a bearded dragon is not receiving or absorbing calcium properly, which devastates its skeletal system by causing the bones to deteriorate. Give your dragon the proper enclosure temperatures and diet to eliminate any chances of it getting this terrible disease. If you believe your lizard could have MBD, immediately take it to a veterinarian. Here are the symptoms of MBD:

Photo Courtesy of Kyra Chiriboga

● Lethargy
● Swelling of the face, mouth, and back legs
● Lack of appetite
● Weakness
● Trembling or twitching of the limbs
● Paralysis or difficulty moving
● Fractures or broken bones
● Bumps along the spine or bones
● Bowed limbs or arched spine

Impaction

Impaction occurs when a bearded dragon has a blockage in its digestion tract caused by an object or from undigested food. Impaction can occur from ingesting substrates with small particles, improper enclosure temperatures or lighting, being fed inappropriate insect sizes, or becoming dehydrated. The number of times a bearded dragon should be eliminating waste depends on its age. A baby bearded dragon should eliminate waste at least once a day, juveniles every other day, and adults at least once a week.

*Photo Courtesy of
Eric Dobo*

If you believe your bearded dragon is suffering from impaction, you can try some things at home, like a gentle massage, a warm bath, and high-water-content foods. Foods with a higher water content that may help move things along include canned pumpkin, banana, watermelon, and apple puree. However, if you cannot resolve your dragon's impaction, don't wait too long before seeing a vet. Symptoms of a bearded dragon experiencing impaction are as follows:

● Loss of mobility
● Lack of appetite
● Lethargy
● Not eliminating waste regularly

Preventing Illnesses

Keeping your bearded dragon and its enclosure as clean as possible reduces the bacteria and viruses that can make your dragon sick. Additionally, you can prevent many illnesses by ensuring the enclosure meets your beardie's temperature, lighting, and humidity requirements. Finally, when you provide your bearded dragon with a balanced and nutritionally adequate diet, you will avoid many illnesses caused by nutritional deficiencies.

Responding Appropriately

A veterinarian has the expertise and resources to treat your bearded dragon accurately and effectively. If you are unsure whether a vet appointment is warranted based on your bearded dragon's symptoms, call your veterinary clinic for their recommendation. As the saying goes, it is always better to be safe than sorry.

When to Take your Bearded Dragon to the Veterinarian

> **“**
>
> *Always listen to the advice of experienced and trusted breeders or suppliers and don't hesitate to contact a veterinarian if you think your dragon is unwell. We find most elderly bearded dragons don't display any obvious health problems, but you should definitely know where your local experienced herpetologist veterinarian is should any health problems occur.*
>
> CHRISTY BRUCKNER
> *Reptile Cymru*
> **”**

Photo Courtesy of Gustav Smedegard

A competent and trusted veterinarian is of great value to your bearded dragon's care and can be a great source of comfort. Taking a bearded dragon to see a veterinarian is not only for when it is experiencing a health issue but also for routine visits. Routine veterinary visits help maintain your bearded dragon's health and well-being so it can live its best life.

Regular Check-ups

Ideally, you should take your new pet to a veterinarian within 48 hours of bringing your beardie home. After that, your bearded dragon should see a veterinarian every six to 12 months. A veterinarian can detect the earliest signs of diseases and infections during regular check-ups. During the examination, your veterinarian will thoroughly examine your bearded dragon to look for abnormalities, check its weight, eyes, mouth, and skeletal system, and look for parasites in a fecal sample. Routine veterinarian check-ups are a great way to be proactive about your bearded dragon's health.

Specific Health Issues and Concerns

As questions and concerns arise, especially for first-time bearded dragon owners, a veterinarian is the best way to seek wise counsel instead of through other sources like the internet or a pet store employee. Often, the advice found online or given by individuals who aren't experts in bearded dragons is inaccurate, outdated, or contradictory, confusing you and delaying your bearded dragon from getting the proper care. The veterinarian will be able to accurately answer the questions about your bearded dragon's diet, enclosure setup, and supplementation. Furthermore, your veterinarian can also answer any other specific health issues or concerns, putting your mind at ease.

Choosing a Veterinarian Experienced with Bearded Dragons

A herpetologist veterinarian will be most qualified to care for your pet and have the right equipment and medication. It's important to find an experienced veterinarian before you get your bearded dragon. If you wait until your pet is sick, you may be wasting precious time searching for a vet in your area instead of taking your bearded dragon to be seen immediately. The Association of Reptilian and Amphibian Veterinarians website is a helpful internet resource that will provide you with a list of qualified veterinarians within a certain radius of your home.

Preparing for a Visit

Bringing your bearded dragon to a veterinary clinic can be stressful, so preparing in advance is essential to keep things running smoothly. Your dragon will need to be secured in a well-ventilated carrier or plastic tub. Lining the carrier or tub with a paper towel or newspaper will make cleaning up any messes easier. Before you take your bearded dragon to the appointment, it is a good idea to turn your vehicle on and let it run to stabilize the internal temperature. You can use extra towels, a warm water bottle, or a heat pack to help keep your bearded dragon's temperature between 65 °F and 90 °F. When you are ready to head to the appointment, find a spot inside your vehicle to put the carrier or container where your lizard will remain secure despite any turns or stops you make.

CHAPTER 6

Breeding Bearded Dragons

Before you decide whether to breed bearded dragons—as this decision should be well-calculated—it is essential to understand the entire breeding process. Much more goes into responsibly breeding bearded dragons than solely putting a male and female bearded dragon together. As gratifying of an experience as this event is, it is also important to understand that you will dedicate months of your life to the cause.

Preparing For Breeding

Several factors need consideration before you begin the breeding process. Although breeding takes several months, preparing certain items and conditioning the pair for breeding in advance is vital for a successful breeding season. The potential breeding pair should be in optimal health, as the whole breeding process is demanding.

Factors to Consider

For the bearded dragons' safety, a trip to the vet is necessary before you begin breeding to determine if they have any infections or illnesses. A veterinarian will ensure the pair are in perfect health and at a healthy weight. If a female bearded dragon is sick and weak during breeding, problems such as egg-binding can occur during pregnancy, becoming life-threatening if not treated in time. More on egg-binding is discussed shortly in this chapter. Additionally, the male and female should be free of any hereditary defects and disorders that would get genetically passed down to offspring. Lastly, since inbreeding can cause abnormalities, health issues, and premature death, the breeding pair should not be from the same clutch.

A male bearded dragon should be at least 18 months old for breeding, and a female should be closer to 24 months old. However, the size of a female dragon is far more important than her age; a female bearded dragon should be at least 18 inches long from snout to tail and 350 grams,

HELPFUL TIP
UVB Lighting

In addition to a heat source and white light, bearded dragons require a specific spectrum of light called UVB. UVB light is critical for calcium absorption because it enables the synthesis of vitamin D3, a vitamin that helps produce a hormone that facilitates calcium absorption. Calcium deficiency has been linked to several health issues for bearded dragons, including bone disease and growth issues. Specific UVB light sources can be purchased at most reptile supply stores. While sunlight provides the necessary UVB light for bearded dragons in the wild, you must provide a reliable source for this in your reptile's indoor enclosure.

and the male should be of equal size and weight. Prematurely breeding a female bearded dragon can result in complications during pregnancy and egg-laying.

Preparing the Habitats and Bearded Dragons

A pre-breeding period is essential to prepare the bearded dragons for a successful breeding season and should take place a couple of months before breeding begins. During the pre-breeding period, each bearded dragon requires a suitable enclosure with the proper setup, as discussed in Chapter 2, to prevent them from fighting with one another. Additionally, they need plenty of nourishing food and water during this time. For two to three weeks before mating, increase the female's calcium

powder supplement from one to three times daily to improve egg development and quality.

Preparing an additional enclosure large enough to house both bearded dragons during mating is necessary. A suitable enclosure size for breeding is five to six feet long and two feet wide or larger. Be sure to provide multiple basking areas in the enclosure, one higher for the male and one lower for the female, and provide different feeding areas. The enclosure needs to meet all the requirements discussed in Chapter 2.

A pseudo-brumation period is critical during pre-breeding for maximum breeding health and fertility and to trigger courtship behaviors shortly after brumation is over. Successfully breeding bearded dragons can still occur without initiating this brumation period, but you can anticipate decreased fertility. You can find more on brumation in Chapter 8.

To encourage your bearded dragons to brumate, imitate the pre-breeding conditions in Australia in each bearded dragon's enclosure. Reduce the lighting cycle to 10 hours of light in the day and 14 hours of darkness for a few months. Additionally, allow daytime temperatures to fall to 75°F to 85°F and nighttime temperature to about 60°F. The best time to create these conditions is in the first two weeks of December, lasting through mid-February.

As the middle of February approaches, return conditions gradually to normal. Within a month of normal temperatures, breeding behaviors will begin. Now, revert to feeding the female one calcium-supplemented meal a day and offer the pair an additional meal daily. Additionally, provide your female with a varied diet of equal parts insects and vegetable matter in different servings until mating occurs.

Creating a Suitable Nesting Box

Since bearded dragons are oviparous, meaning they produce young by laying eggs, and are burrow nesters, it will be necessary to create a nesting box—sometimes called a laying box or digging box. A nesting box is a shallow, open container filled with a moist and warm substrate that a female bearded dragon can dig a nest in to deposit her eggs. The best time to create and prepare a suitable nesting box is before you begin breeding your bearded dragons. If you do not provide this for your female bearded dragon or fail to provide an appropriate substrate, she won't deposit the eggs, subjecting her to egg-binding or a difficult birth.

The ideal nesting box size is large enough for your bearded dragon to move freely and comfortably and is deep enough to hold nine to 12 inches of substrate. A suitable nesting box can be made from a plastic storage container with part of the lid removed, measuring 18 inches long, 12 inches wide, and 12 inches deep. Nesting boxes can be placed inside or right outside the female's enclosure. For a nesting box placed outside an enclosure, use a container deep enough to prevent the female bearded dragon from climbing out and keep the nesting box at approximately 80°F by clamping a heat bulb to the side of the box.

Fill the nesting box with sterile, pesticide-free sand and topsoil at least nine inches deep. You will need to experiment with the sand, topsoil, and water ratio until you achieve a consistency that resembles the sand used to make a sandcastle at the beach. Some use a 50/50 mixture, while others use an 80/20. The overall goal is to provide a substrate in the nesting box that retains moisture well and is damp enough to keep form but is not waterlogged.

The Breeding Process

Whether you are a first-time bearded dragon keeper or otherwise, breeding bearded dragons rarely results in any problems. During the breeding process, you should be present to assist in the breeding stages, including brumation, courtship, mating, and egg-laying. Keep in mind that it is possible for female dragons to lay multiple clutches throughout a year after successfully mating one time. It is a good idea to postpone any trips, vacations, or holidays and not to be absent for long periods in a day for the entire breeding duration.

Bearded Dragon Breeding Behavior

Once the brumation period is over, dragon behaviors will return to normal. Now you need to introduce your male and female to one another in the designated enclosure for breeding. Their introduction should be slow and demands vigilant watching of body language and behavior. If, at any time, their interactions become too aggressive and injury occurs, the pair will need to go into separate enclosures for a brief time. With each dragon separated, rearrange the contents inside the breeding enclosure and reintroduce the beardies.

The breeding pair will begin to exhibit signs that indicate they are ready for mating within three weeks to a month after coming out of brumation. A male prepared to mate will display specific behaviors to attract the female dragon and signal his desire to copulate. These behaviors include frequent head bobbing, nipping, biting, and showing a jet-black beard. As he chases after the female, she will attempt to run away at first and may signal submission

FUN FACT
Hatchlings

Newly hatched beardies are called "hatchlings." Bearded dragon hatchlings can be as small as three inches and four to six grams. Adult beardies can reach 16 to 24 inches long and weigh up to a pound.

by arm waving. After a few days, your female bearded dragon will no longer run away and will use her upper torso to do movements that look like push-ups, signaling she is ready to mate.

Monitoring the Breeding Process

During the breeding process, it is essential to closely monitor your bearded dragons since courtship and mating are physically taxing and problems can occur. The male will bite the female's neck to hold her in place and twist his tail around hers during copulation to prevent her from running away. Copulation is brief, lasting approximately 30 seconds to two minutes. Once the dragons have successfully mated, they can return to separate enclosures.

Intervening When Necessary

Not all breeding pairs are compatible, so certain circumstances may require you to intervene. One case that can warrant an intervention is a female unwilling to mate that persists for several days. Likewise, you will need to intervene in cases where the male is reluctant to mate with the female, as an unwilling male can attack a female and severely injure her. The last case requiring your intervention is if a male bearded dragon bites other places other than the female's neck during copulation, causing injury.

Caring for Eggs and Hatchlings

After a successful mating session, your female bearded dragon will begin to experience changes to her body in the next few weeks, indicating she is gravid or carrying eggs. During this exciting time, your female bearded dragon will need extra pampering as she will work hard to develop a clutch averaging 15 to 30 eggs. Caring for the eggs and the hatchlings that will soon be born is a delicate process.

Creating an Incubation Box with Substrate

Despite four weeks or more between mating and egg-laying, you will want an incubation box ready before your bearded dragon lays her eggs. An incubating box is a container with a tight-fitting lid large enough to hold the number of eggs in a clutch. The box also needs an absorbent substrate at the bottom to provide moisture for the eggs. You can use a sturdy plastic container with a lid, such as a large plastic food storage container, a sizable plastic sweater box, or a plastic shoebox to create an incubation box at home. Materials such as cardboard or wood do not make satisfactory boxes as they will absorb the moisture from the substrate. The container's upper sides and lid will need small ventilation holes.

The incubation box will need a substrate that can hold moisture well to maintain humidity and have a relatively coarse texture to prevent eggs from rolling around. The most commonly used substrate is vermiculite, commonly found at local gardening stores or online. The substrate should measure at least two inches in depth and will need water added. The water-to-substrate ratio for vermiculite is 1:1, calculated by weight, not volume. Getting the moisture correct is imperative, so be sure to follow the instructions closely.

Egg-laying

As your beardie's belly becomes engorged with many eggs, it's a good idea to monitor her closely and watch for signs of illness or complications like egg-binding. Expect egg-laying to occur four to six weeks after successful mating. Signs your bearded dragon is ready to lay eggs include irritability, restlessness, trying to dig, a decreased appetite for several days, and scratching at tank walls. However, if your bearded dragon has failed to lay her eggs within the specified time, has stopped eating, is straining to lay her eggs, or cannot find a spot to lay her eggs (despite you providing a nesting box), these indicate egg-binding, and she will need to get to a vet quickly.

Once you witness behaviors that signal the bearded dragon is ready to lay her eggs, place the nesting box inside or outside her enclosure and place her inside the nesting box. Typically, instinct will take over, and within a couple of hours, she will dig in multiple places with great determination until she meticulously creates a spot to lay her eggs. If her nesting box is outside her enclosure and she doesn't lay her eggs within a few hours, return her to her enclosure and repeat the process the next day. The eggs can vary in length and shape but are roughly one-inch long and oval.

After your female bearded dragon lays her clutch of eggs, which is around 15-30 eggs, carefully excavate them and transfer them to the incubation box in the same position you found them. Some keepers mark the side facing up with a pencil to keep things organized. Bury about half to two-thirds of the eggs in the substrate and put the leftover eggs on top. However, before placing the rest of the eggs on top, it is a good idea to make a small indentation in the sand with your finger or a spoon for each egg to prevent the eggs from accidentally rolling. Every egg should be spaced far enough apart in the incubation box not to touch each other and to allow room for the eggs to swell as they absorb water during their development. Securely place the lid on the container; after this point, the eggs should remain untouched—never turned—and undisturbed.

Providing the Right Temperature and Humidity for Eggs

For the eggs to remain living and for proper development, they need to be incubated at a constant and regulated temperature. Although there are a couple of methods to do this successfully, the best and most convenient way to guarantee a fixed and controlled temperature and humidity level is by using a commercial incubator. The temperature needed for incubation is between 82.4°F to 86°F with a humidity level of 75%. It's important to place the incubator in a room with a temperature lower than the set temperature on the incubator to avoid temperatures rising too high. Incorrect temperatures, even a couple of degrees, will result in damaged or terminated eggs. To maintain the correct humidity levels, ensure the substrate stays moist and that the incubator's water container has water in it at all times.

Choosing a Commercial Incubator

The incubator you decide on will significantly impact the quality of the eggs and the developing fetuses. The best commercial incubators are big enough to incubate a large capacity of eggs and are lightweight, durable, easy to use, and designed for reptiles. The incubator should have good heat and humidity retention and have built-in and trusted features like a thermometer and hygrometer to control heating and temperature, including a fan for air circulation. Additionally, look for an incubator that allows for the adjustment or detachment of the levels or layers so any size incubation box can fit inside. Building plans are available online to make an incubator at home if you so choose.

Hatching Eggs

Hatchlings will begin emerging from their eggs after an incubation period of about 55 to 75 days when incubated at 85°F. About 48 hours before eggs are to hatch, they will deflate and collapse as the baby bearded dragons use the yolk and fluid inside the eggs. It is also not uncommon to see slits in the eggshells at this time. Usually, eggs hatch within 24 to 72 hours after that. As tempting as it may be, do not pull a hatchling out of its egg during any part of the hatching phase, as this could lead to death. Hatchlings measure three to four inches long from their tail to their snout and weigh three to six grams. Once the hatchlings have emerged, they should be left in their incubation box until you observe them being active. After this time, moving them to an enclosure setup to meet their needs is safe.

Feeding Hatchlings

From the day they are born, baby bearded dragons can do everything independently. They will begin eating on their own within the first 24 hours and need multiple feedings of appropriately sized insects and a leafy green salad every day. Each hatchling can eat 20 to 40 small insects

Photo Courtesy of Vincent Graves

daily, so ensure you have enough insects on hand to feed them all. Providing frequent meals and avoiding overfeeding is especially important to prevent gastrointestinal blockages.

For the next six months, you can't skip any feedings, and if, for any reason, you can't fulfill your feeding duties, you will need to find a trusted person who can take over this responsibility. Revisit Chapter 3 for a more detailed explanation of the nutrition and diet requirements.

Providing the Right Enclosure Setup and Care

It's a good idea to divide hatchlings into smaller groups of five and provide multiple enclosures. Enclosures should be set up similarly to the one described for baby bearded dragons in Chapter 2. It's important to note that baby bearded dragons will significantly benefit from being misted with water a few times throughout the day, as they often get dehydrated quickly. Additionally, they should be soaked in lukewarm water every other day for fifteen minutes.

Monitoring Growth and Development

Monitoring your hatchlings' growth rate is crucial to ensure they are growing properly and are putting on weight as they should. In the first two months, healthy babies grow about one to three inches per month and can gain up to 40 grams. If any hatchling is not developing correctly or fails to put on the appropriate amount of weight, it will need to be seen by a veterinarian.

CHAPTER 7

Fun Activities and Enrichment

As a new bearded dragon owner, I was worried about finding fun activities and enrichment that would bring excitement to our bearded dragon's life. After digging a little deeper, I was relieved to find many activities and items to nourish my bearded dragon's brain and encourage movement. Providing fun activities and enrichment for your bearded dragon will directly impact and enhance its quality of life.

Photo Courtesy of
Cortney Farr

Providing Mental and Physical Stimulation

All bearded dragons greatly benefit from different experiences and activities, especially from the ones outside their enclosure. Mental and physical stimulation are different terms, but both are equally important and go hand in hand.

Importance of Mental and Physical Stimulation

Boredom in a bearded dragon often manifests through behaviors like glass surfing and restlessness. Boredom can lead to unhappiness or even depression and can cause your dragon not to be very interactive or active. Providing your bearded dragon with mentally and physically stimulating activities and enrichment is the antidote to boredom. Some activities are especially beneficial as they stimulate your bearded dragon mentally and physically all in one activity.

Interaction and Exploration

Bearded dragons love to explore, and an outdoor adventure is a fun way to see your dragon interact and behave in a natural setting. During outdoor excursions, your bearded dragon will be alert and interested in everything outside. It will also greatly benefit from natural vitamin D from the sun. Before heading out, you should be mindful of the temperature; it should be at least 70°F, with a humidity level lower than 60%. It is essential to watch your pet closely to prevent it from eating things it shouldn't, like rocks, plants,

FUN FACT
Like A Mood Ring

Like the ubiquitous mood rings of the 1990s, beardies can change color based on their mood or temperature. In general, beardies have a light and warm coloration when happy and turn darker colors when cold or stressed.

*Photo Courtesy of
Shalynn Tanner*

and insects. It's also a good idea to put a harness and leash designed for bearded dragons on your lizard to keep it close by.

Toys and Other Enrichment Items

There are many toys and items you can use for enrichment. A laser pointer cat owners often use for their pets to chase can stimulate your bearded dragon's mind as it chases after the red dot. You can also give your bearded dragon small balls, cat toys, stuffed animals, and rubber ducks.

Identifying and Meeting Individual Needs and Preferences

DID YOU KNOW?
Domesticated Bearded Dragon Species

Did you know that out of the eight species of bearded dragons, four have emerged as popular choices for reptile enthusiasts as domesticated pets? The top most common pet species of bearded dragons are:

- Central or Inland Bearded Dragon (Pogona vitticeps)
- Rankin's Dragon (Pogona henrylawsoni)
- Dwarf Bearded Dragon (Pogona minor minor)
- Mitchell's or Black Soil Bearded Dragon (Pogona minor mitchelli)

The remaining four species have not gained the same popularity as domesticated pets primarily due to their rarity, specific habitat requirements, or more challenging care needs. They can require specialized care, such as specific temperature or humidity conditions, making them less suitable for the average reptile owner.

As you get to know your bearded dragon well, you can customize the enrichment items and activities to meet its needs and preferences. For example, if you know your bearded dragon loves going outside to explore, you can apply that information to situations when it wants time out of its enclosure. Doing so will meet your bearded dragon's need for time out of its enclosure and also its preference for what it enjoys doing the most.

Ideas for Fun Activities and Toys

Many commercially made reptile toys and activities are available to keep your bearded dragon's mind stimulated and engaged. Toys like puzzle feeders and treat balls provide great mental and/or physical enrichment for your bearded dragon. Additionally, hide boxes, hammocks, and climbing structures may not seem like toys, but they are very exciting for your bearded dragon.

Making Your Own Toys and Activities

Everyday household items can quickly become toys for your bearded dragon. For example, you can use crinkled paper formed into a loose

Photo Courtesy of
Nicole Casterline

ball for your bearded dragon to push around with its nose. Bearded dragons love things that make sounds, so things like bubble wrap, wrapping paper, and newspaper will keep them entertained for a while. Lastly, medium- to large-sized bouncy balls make an excellent toy for your bearded dragon.

There are many activities you can create at home for your pet. Creating a beardie burrito is a fun activity to do with your bearded dragon. It involves wrapping your bearded dragon in a small blanket, similar to swaddling a baby. You can also construct an obstacle course or a maze using cardboard boxes, paper towels, and toilet paper rolls. Another idea is to create a dig box for your bearded dragon using a large container like a cardboard box and filling it with something fun, like leaves or paper scraps. Additional activities include nature walks, exploring rooms in your house, baths, climbing a cat tower, snuggling, swimming in pools, and window watching.

Photo Courtesy of Amber Harris

Choosing Safe and Appropriate Toys and Activities

When choosing the toys for your bearded dragon, they should never have sharp edges or be small enough to be eaten, like marbles or small rubber balls. Choose toys without feathers or small parts that your bearded dragon could eat. Furthermore, the activities for your bearded dragon should never involve leaving your beardie unattended or dangerous activities that could cause injury.

Creating a Naturalistic Habitat for Your Bearded Dragon

Creating a naturalistic habitat is an excellent method to make an enclosure look more visually appealing and provide a bearded dragon with enrichment opportunities to behave as it naturally would. You can create a naturalistic environment in your enclosure by including plants, natural pieces, and decorations that resemble the ones found in a dragon's natural habitat. A realistic setup will make your bearded dragon feel at home and provide it with a space it enjoys spending time in.

*Photo Courtesy of
Shalynn Tanner*

Providing Plants, Branches, Rocks, and Other Natural Materials

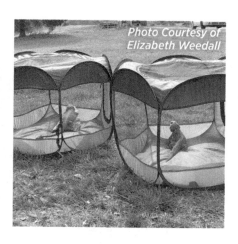

Photo Courtesy of Elizabeth Weedall

The key to creating a natural-istic habitat is using materials that look most similar to what is found in Australia. Natural materials like dried grasses, twigs and branches, rocks, driftwood, grape vines, and cork bark pieces work great to cre-ate a habitat that looks natural. Incorporating living plants is also a great way to add natural elements as long as they don't increase humidity to an unhealthy level. Adding different textures and an Australian desert ter-rarium background helps to bring depth and contrast to your setup. If it is within your budget, purchase a ledge-style background for an even more naturalistic habitat. Using a more natural substrate like brown reptile carpet, reptile sand mats, natural color tile, or store-bought arid bio-active substrates also adds to the natural look.

Photo Courtesy of Kaley Whelpley

Arranging the Habitat in an Attractive and Stimulating Way

Arrange the contents in the enclosure so they allow your bearded dragon to move easily from one object to the next. For example, by placing the climbing structure next to a hammock, your bearded dragon can use the

Photo Courtesy of Kyra Chiriboga

structure to get onto the hammock that it otherwise couldn't reach from the floor of the enclosure. You will want to maximize the space without adding too many items inside the enclosure, so your bearded dragon still has ample room to move around. Additionally, occasionally changing or rearranging the contents inside the enclosure stimulates your bearded dragon's mind as it has to relearn where things are.

Maintaining a Naturalistic Habitat

To successfully maintain a naturalistic habitat for your bearded dragon, cleaning and disinfection of the contents within the enclosure, including artificial plants, is necessary. Follow the detailed guidelines found in Chapter 2, "Maintaining the Habitat."

CHAPTER 8

Common Bearded Dragon Behaviors

Bearded dragons have their own unique set of behaviors they use to communicate their mood, health, and feelings. Your bearded dragon entirely depends on you to interpret its behaviors and respond. The more you understand your bearded dragon's behaviors, the healthier and happier your bearded dragon will be.

Understanding Bearded Dragon Behaviors

> "
>
> *Bearded dragons have a lot of behaviors that might seem abnormal but are actually perfectly normal, such as sitting with their mouths open, having a black or puffed-up beard, not drinking water directly, scratching, digging, and climbing anything available. I often get questions from new owners about all those things and am happy to put people's minds at ease. Obvious problems to look for would be not eating at all after the first day or two, not being able to walk or move correctly, having any injuries, and things of that nature.*
>
> CHRISTY BRUCKNER
>
> *Reptile Cymru*
>
> "

An important part of responsibly owning a bearded dragon is understanding its behaviors. You can tell a lot from the behaviors your bearded dragon uses as they give much insight into how your beardie is feeling. It will also provide a basis for discerning between healthy behaviors and when something is wrong.

HELPFUL TIP
A Language of Their Own

Bearded dragons don't vocalize in the same way that humans or mammalian pets might. Instead, these reptiles are relatively quiet, making only a handful of soft hissing or burping sounds. So how do they communicate? A bearded dragon's language consists primarily of color displays, postural changes, and arm waving. For example, male bearded dragons often engage in a behavior called "head bobbing," which can be a way to establish dominance or to attract a female during mating season.

Natural Behaviors

Natural behaviors are ones that bearded dragons do instinctually in the wild. They use various forms of communication to respond to, interact with, and control their environment. Understanding these natural behaviors and their reasoning is the only way to enter your animal's world. The following are several common behaviors and why bearded dragons may use them to communicate.

Blackening of the Beard

Bearded dragons can turn their beard black when feeling excited or stressed. They may also display a black beard when they have high energy, like after brumation, during the mating season, or in a new environment. A black beard can also signal illness if accompanied by other symptoms

Photo Courtesy of Trish Wood

like lethargy, appetite loss, and mouth swelling. In this case, veterinary care is necessary.

Beard Flaring

Bearded dragons will flare and puff out their beards during stress or when feeling threatened. At the same time, their beard can also turn black. Sometimes they become stressed when foreign items are placed into their environment, if temperatures or lighting inside their enclosure are incorrect, or if another pet is nearby.

Photo Courtesy of Jerry Hayden

Arm Waving

In what looks like an arm wave, bearded dragons will intentionally lift one of their arms above their head and then gently circle it back around toward the ground. Bearded dragons do this behavior quickly, sometimes slowly, or it can also appear choppy. A bearded dragon will wave as a sign of submission or when caught off guard by sudden movements, people, pets, or loud noises. This behavior is also commonly practiced by female bearded dragons during mating. If you see your bearded dragon wave, give your dragon some space because it may feel threatened.

Head Bobbing

Bearded dragons, primarily males, bob their heads up and down quickly to demonstrate excitement or aggression. For example, male bearded dragons use head bobbing to get the female's attention during breeding or to intimidate and threaten other male dragons by declaring dominance. Fast bobbing usually serves as a warning, while slow bobs signify submission.

Color Changing

Bearded dragons are capable of subtly changing the color of their bodies. They can also target specific body areas, such as their head, neck, beard, and tail. A bearded dragon may change colors during handling or as its body temperature changes. Additionally, beardies often change to a darker color if they feel threatened or upset, but a pale bearded dragon usually indicates it is calm and relaxed.

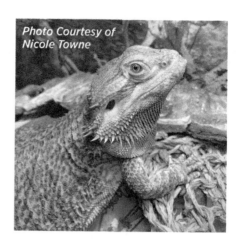

Photo Courtesy of Nicole Towne

Digging

Bearded dragons love to dig, which is part of their natural behavior. However, digging can also be for many other reasons. Digging around at the bottom of their enclosure can signal they are about to brumate, there are improper enclosure temperatures, or it's time for gravid females to lay their eggs.

Photo Courtesy of Elizabeth Weedall

Gaping

It is natural for bearded dragons to have their mouths wide open for an extended period, mainly while basking. Holding the mouth open prevents overheating

Photo Courtesy of Holly Abernathy

and is comparable to why a dog pants. However, if your dragon's mouth is open while it's on the cooler side of the enclosure, you should check the terrarium's temperatures to ensure they are correct. Additionally, rapid and shallow breathing, accompanied by the gaping behavior, could signal an upper respiratory infection. If this appears to be the case, you will need to seek veterinary care as soon as possible.

Shedding

Like snakes, bearded dragons also shed their skin from time to time. It is common to see a shedding bearded dragon bulge out its eyes to stretch the skin and loosen it. You may also see your bearded dragon rub on things inside its enclosure to help get the shed off. With shedding can come the loss of appetite due to discomfort or itching. To help your bearded dragon with shedding, give it several soakings in warm water throughout the week and use a soft toothbrush to gently scrub its body, paying close attention to limbs, toes, and tail.

Photo Courtesy of Nicole Rowe

Brumation

Brumation is a period of inactivity for bearded dragons, usually beginning in November or early December. Shortened days, lower temperatures, and instincts can trigger a bearded dragon to brumate. Not all bearded dragons go through brumation, but for those who do, it usually lasts from a few weeks to months. If your bearded dragon doesn't enter a state of brumation naturally, there is no need to force it to, except for breeding. Sick, baby, and young bearded dragons should never be forced into brumation.

During this dormancy period, bearded dragons will become sluggish and lethargic and may not enjoy being handled. You will notice that they are not as interested in eating or will not eat at all. Additionally, they will hide, sleep longer, and no longer bask under their light. If your bearded dragon does brumate, there are a few things you can do to help:

Photo Courtesy of Kendra Cummings

- Keep the lights on for eight to 10 hours a day.
- Reduce the enclosure temperature to about 65°F.
- Ensure there is plenty of water available.
- Provide a space for the beardie to hide.

Flattening Body

Bearded dragons will noticeably flatten their bodies out, giving them a round appearance with bigger and sharper scales. They may display this behavior when they feel threatened to protect against predators and to make

Photo Courtesy of Leslie Vicars

them look visually unappealing. Conversely, some will flatten out during basking in the sun to increase their surface area.

Responding in an Appropriate and Beneficial Way

Identifying and proactively resolving any issues that arise while caring for your bearded dragon before they have a negative impact is crucial. While you can prevent most problems from occurring through proper care and enclosure conditions and by regular and appropriate handling, not all issues can be avoided. Paying attention to early warning signs that indicate a problem is developing is essential.

Common Behavior Problems and How to Address Them

Understanding behavior problems is as crucial as understanding natural behaviors in a bearded dragon. Since bearded dragons communicate, defend, and protect themselves through body language, they will use aggressive behaviors as a first line of defense to communicate dislikes when feeling scared, threatened, unwell, or in pain.

Aggression

Defensive behaviors such as posturing, open-mouth threatening, head-bobbing, darkening and flaring beard, and hissing, are typical behaviors in bearded dragons experiencing stress, feeling threatened, or in pain. Sudden aggressive behaviors in male bearded dragons can sometimes be linked to the  arrival of mating season. It's also common to see bearded dragons temporarily display aggression when they are outside, which can be seen in even the tamest bearded dragons.

Biting

Bearded dragons don't usually bite, but it can still happen when they feel stressed, threatened, or in pain. A bite is often a last-ditch attempt to scare the threat away and create distance between the bearded dragon and the danger. Still, they will usually demonstrate other less aggressive behaviors before biting. A bearded dragon may also attempt to bite its owner if it is not properly socialized. Once your bearded dragon realizes that you and your hand are not a threat, it will stop trying to bite you. In the meantime, wear protective gloves until your beardie gets comfortable with you.

Glass Surfing

Bearded dragons may run back and forth along the bottom of their enclosure or stand on their hind legs to try to run up the side to get out. This problematic behavior stems mainly from boredom and wanting to get out to explore. Your bearded dragon may need more time out of its enclosure to stretch its legs and see new things, or it may need a larger aquarium. Less common reasons for this behavior include stress arising from new decorations, unsanitary enclosure conditions, or incorrect enclosure lighting and temperatures. Glass surfing can result in injury

from continually rubbing the face, abdomen, and feet over the enclosure, so getting to the bottom of this behavior is always a good idea.

Preventing Behavior Problems

Identifying and addressing behavior problems are the first steps to preventing and correcting them. The best way to avoid behavior problems in your bearded dragon is by providing proper enclosure setup and diet, care, handling, and interactions. Additionally, preventative health care is another important way to prevent illness and infections that can lead to behavior problems.

Regular Handling and Interaction

Regular handling and interactions in an appropriate manner are beneficial for your bearded dragon's mental health. Bearded dragons that aren't handled regularly often experience stress anytime interactions or handling are necessary. Consequently, regular interactions encourage healthy behaviors, build confidence and trust, and prevent behaviors associated with anxiety and fear. Not excessively handling your bearded dragon is equally essential, as it can lead to stress.

Suitable Environment and Diet

Providing your bearded dragon with a suitable environment and diet is imperative to prevent behavior problems. For that reason, ensure you feed your bearded dragon a fresh, varied, plant-based diet with appropriate insects, and provide plenty of clean water. Similarly, ensure your bearded dragon has a spacious enough enclosure to move around in and is set up with the appropriate lighting and temperatures to avoid stress, illness, boredom, and associated behavior problems.

FUN FACT
Affection

Bearded dragons are delightful pets due in part to their ability to show affection to their owners. Although beardies are not as expressive as domestic dogs and cats, they have been known to favor their owners by remaining calm in their favorite human's lap.

CHAPTER 9

Common Questions and Concerns

I t is normal to have questions and concerns as you set about raising your bearded dragon, especially in the first year. Below are common questions and concerns among new bearded dragon owners.

Frequently Asked Questions

Can more than one bearded dragon be housed together?

This question is a controversial topic. The short answer is no. Longtime bearded dragon owners and breeders Mark Dohmen and Katie Grove from Midwest Dragons in Florida never recommend cohabitation, and for good reason. They believe *"the biggest problem with cohabitation is the establishment of the hierarchy in which one of the dragons becomes dominant and the other becomes*

DID YOU KNOW?

Surf's Up

When threatened or stressed, bearded dragons have a unique defense mechanism called "glass surfing" or "glass dancing." This behavior includes repeatedly running or rubbing against the sides of their enclosure. While many owners may initially find this behavior endearing, it can indicate stress or a desire to escape perceived danger.

Photo Courtesy of Andi Smith

lethargic, may get sick, stop eating, be attacked by the other, and can even die." Mark and Katie raise their dragons "in individual enclosures so they never get nipped by other dragons. They are raised having lots of confidence, no competition for food, and physically complete with all toes and tails."

What do I need to purchase before bringing my new pet home?

You will need the following supplies to raise a healthy and happy lizard.

Housing
- A 40-gallon enclosure or larger (with a ventilated screen lid, if applicable)
- A heat/basking bulb with a fixture
- A UVB bulb with a fixture
- A water and food dish
- A hideaway
- A basking platform or rock

- Some form of substrate
- A hygrometer (digital is best)
- At least two temperature gauges (digital is best)
- A thermostat or dimmer
- Water conditioner
- A noncontact temperature gun
- Decorations (optional)
- Background (optional)

Food
- Feeder insects
- Feeder insect food
- Vegetables
- Multivitamin supplement
- Calcium supplement
- Tongs or tweezers (optional)

Cleaning
- Cleaning solution
- Rubber gloves

Photo Courtesy of
Maggie Miller

How do I care for my bearded dragon during a power outage?

Taking steps to keep your bearded dragon warm during a power outage is only necessary when the temperature in your home drops below 65°F. Keeping your lizard warm until power is restored is especially important if you live somewhere that experiences winter. You can warm your bearded dragon by wrapping it in a blanket and using your body to provide heat or by sitting in your car—just be sure to warm the vehicle up ahead of time. Heat packs wrapped in a sock also serve as a great way to keep your pet warm.

FUN FACT
Can You See What I See?

Bearded dragons have excellent eyesight, with a significantly more expansive range of vision than humans. In addition to the eyes on either side of their head, bearded dragons possess a third eye used exclusively to detect light, temperature, and shadows. While this third eye, the parietal eye, can't perceive clear images like the other two eyes, it helps detect seasonal changes and process critical information about the bearded dragon's environment.

What do I do if the humidity levels are too high in my bearded dragon's enclosure?

It is necessary to reduce humidity levels in your bearded dragon's enclosure if they rise above the recommended 30% to 40%. You can lower humidity levels by improving the airflow in the enclosure by adding a fan to the room and using a dehumidifier. If that doesn't lower humidity levels, try moving the tank to a room with lower humidity. Additionally, if you have living plants or a loose substrate that attracts moisture in your enclosure, try artificial plants and a different substrate instead. You can also try moving the water bowl to the cool side if it isn't

Photo Courtesy of
Stacey Griego

already there, and add a rice sock (a sock filled with rice that is tied shut) inside the enclosure to help absorb some moisture.

Where should I put my bearded dragon's enclosure?

Where you put your bearded dragon's enclosure is vital to keeping your pet healthy. The best spot to put the enclosure is in a well-lit, climate-controlled room, away from direct sunlight or cold, drafty air. You should avoid placing the enclosure in a cold basement room or garage. Make sure it is out of the reach of children and pets.

Is sand a suitable substrate in my bearded dragon's enclosure?

Using sand as a substrate for a bearded dragon's enclosure is controversial. The debate is centered around the belief that sand can cause impaction in a bearded dragon when ingested accidentally or intentionally. Those in favor of using sand for a substrate argue that not all types of sand substrates are harmful and that specific sand substrates will not cause impaction in a healthy dragon. They recommend using play sand, reptile sand, and other sands made of quartz designed for reptiles. However, most experts and keepers unanimously agree that sand advertised as calcium sand or vitamin sand should be avoided because of a long history of causing blockages in bearded dragons' intestines. If you aren't sure if sand is the right choice for your beardie's enclosure, ask a veterinarian or another trusted source.

Can I feed my bearded dragon commercially prepared food instead of live insects and vegetables?

No, experts and longtime bearded dragon keepers do not recommend swapping out vegetables and live insects for commercial foods. Bearded dragons need a diet that closely matches their natural one to meet their nutritional requirements best.

Can a bearded dragon be fed pinky mice?

Yes, but it depends on the age of the beardie. Pinky mice, one to three days old, are only suitable for adult beardies. Since pinky mice are high in fat and protein, they are great for underweight dragons, gravid females, or females that have just laid a clutch of eggs. Pinkies should only be offered to an adult bearded dragon once a month.

Can a bearded dragon be a picky eater?

Yes, some bearded dragons can be picky eaters from the start and prefer certain foods over others. On the other hand, sometimes a bearded dragon can suddenly become particular about foods—most commonly vegetables—because its owner feeds it too many insects or treats or does not provide a balanced and varied diet. If your bearded dragon is picky, try offering different kinds of vegetables and holding back on too many insects. However, if a

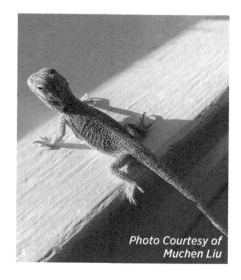

Photo Courtesy of Muchen Liu

Photo Courtesy of Christina Grace

bearded dragon is losing weight, it should be seen by a veterinarian.

Why is calcium powder so controversial?

The debate revolves around whether or not insects should be dusted with calcium powder containing vitamin D3 or without. Those who support using calcium powder without vitamin D3, like Renzo from OlympicBeardedDragon, believe that bearded dragons get sufficient vitamin D3 from the UVB lamp, assuming it is of high quality and the proper strength. They claim that too much vitamin D3 will cause malformations if a bearded dragon gets the vitamin both from the powder and the UVB lamp. Conversely, those who believe calcium powder should contain vitamin D3 say beardies require the vitamin to prevent diseases and illnesses associated with a calcium deficiency. If you are unsure which powder is better for your bearded dragon, consult a veterinarian or another reliable person.

Can I sprinkle calcium powder on my bearded dragon's salad instead of dusting insects?

Dusting insects with calcium instead of sprinkling it on a salad is always the preferred method, as it provides a better way to monitor your bearded dragon's calcium intake. Still, if you alternate the days you feed insects to your bearded dragon, on those days, sprinkling two small pinches of calcium powder on top of a salad is acceptable.

How long can a bearded dragon be out of its enclosure?

The length of time a bearded dragon can safely be out of its enclosure depends on age. If your bearded dragon is older than a hatchling, it can safely be out of its enclosure for five to 15 minutes at a time, several times daily. In case of an emergency, a beardie can be out of its enclosure for 24 hours if temperatures do not fall below 65°F.

Can a new bearded dragon be handled as soon as it gets to its new home?

No, a bearded dragon should be handled minimally in the first couple of days to keep stress levels low and to allow your lizard to get acclimated to its new home first. After a couple of days, ease into handling your new pet and slowly establish a trusting relationship and bond. Although there is no hard-and-fast rule for how often a bearded dragon should be handled daily, about two to four sessions a day for up to 15 minutes each session is a good idea to prevent stress from excessive handling.

Can I contract salmonella from my bearded dragon?

Yes, most reptiles are carriers of salmonella. The best way to lower your risk of contracting salmonella is by practicing good hygiene and following a few rules.

- Always wash your hands after handling a bearded dragon or touching contents that have been in contact with the reptile.
- Keep the enclosure as clean as possible.
- Bathe your bearded dragon regularly.
- Avoid kissing your bearded dragon or sharing food with it.

- Supervise children to ensure they don't put their fingers in their mouths during handling.
- Dedicate a specific bin for baths.
- Sanitize tubs, sinks, and surfaces your bearded dragon encounters.

How long should my bearded dragon be for its age?

Age (Months)	Size (Inches)
0–1	3–4
2	5–9
3	8–11
4	9–12
5	11–16
6	11–18
8	13–20
12+	16–24

How can a female bearded dragon lay eggs without a male present?

A female bearded dragon can lay infertile eggs without a male due to facultative parthenogenesis. Facultative parthenogenesis is the ability to reproduce asexually. If you suspect your female bearded dragon is gravid with infertile eggs, you should provide her with a nesting box, as discussed in Chapter 6. If you're unsure whether the eggs are fertile, you can determine the difference between fertile and infertile eggs through candling. Candling involves gently holding a small light, like a flashlight, up to an egg in a dark room to look for an embryo. The embryo will look like a slightly pink dot with veins extending out. You will need to dispose of infertile eggs.

How long can a bearded dragon go without UVB?

A bearded dragon can go about two days without a UVB light before this becomes detrimental to its health. It is always a good idea to have a spare bulb at home in case a UVB bulb unexpectedly stops working.

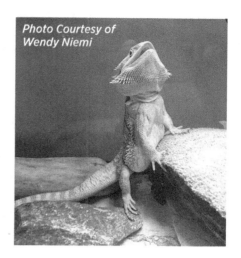

Photo Courtesy of Wendy Niemi

How many baths should I give my bearded dragon in a week?

There is no set number for how many baths a bearded dragon should get. However, owners should bathe their reptiles at least once a week. Increasing the baths to three or four a week is a good idea during shedding and in the summer. The length of time your bearded dragon should soak in the water varies depending on the lizard's tolerance for baths, but ideally, baths should last between five to 20 minutes and even longer throughout shedding.

How can you determine if a bearded dragon is male or female?

The easiest and most popular way to sex a bearded dragon is to look for two hemipenile bulges running vertically on each side of the base of its tail. This method can be done in an eight-month-old or older dragon. To check for these bulges, while a bearded dragon is flat on its stomach, gently lift its tail at a 90-degree angle. If you see two bulges on both sides of the base, it is a male. If you see one bulge located in the middle, it is a female. Other noticeable differences between males and females are that males have larger heads, thicker tails, and more prominent femoral pores along the underside of their thighs.

How often do bearded dragons shed?

From birth to six months old, a beardie will shed weekly. As its growth rate begins to slow, starting at around six months old, the bearded dragon will shed every few weeks for the next six months. By the time the lizard reaches 12 months old, it will shed once every few months, and at 18 months and on, it will only shed a couple of times a year.

What do bearded dragon feces look like? Do they smell?

Healthy bearded dragon feces will be firm and brown and have a log-like shape with a white or yellow portion at the end called urate. Like birds, bearded dragons expel fecal matter and urate at the same time. A healthy bearded dragon will not go longer than one week without eliminating waste. Their feces are foul-smelling, but they can be even more malodorous if the lizard has parasites or has eaten something that doesn't agree with it.

Addressing Common Concerns and Misconceptions

There are many misconceptions encompassing bearded dragons and their care. You can especially find them on the Internet, where any inexperienced person has the opportunity to give information or advice. The following are four common misconceptions.

Misconception #1

Bearded dragons can be kept in small enclosures

Bearded dragons will not thrive in a small enclosure. They require a large enclosure with ample space so their 16- to 24-inch bodies can move freely. The enclosure must be wide enough for them to turn around easily. Additionally, a large enclosure is necessary because it allows for a temperature gradient to exist, which is required to properly care for a bearded dragon. A large enclosure will also help prevent behavior problems associated with stress and boredom by allowing enough space to add enriching items like hides, climbing structures, hammocks, decorations, etc.

Misconception #2

Bearded dragons can be legally owned in any state

Unfortunately, bearded dragons aren't legal to have in all 50 states. Many states require a permit to own a bearded dragon, while others have put a partial or complete ban on them. For the states requiring a permit, the person applying must be at least 16 years old or will need parental/guardian consent.

Misconception #3

Bearded dragons are expensive to keep

The cost of owning a bearded dragon adds up quickly but is similar to the cost of owning a cat or dog. The one-time cost for the habitat and setup is around $300, but that number can be much higher depending on which type of enclosures, equipment, and decorations you choose.

Photo Courtesy of Skylar Hooper

Expect to pay between $45 to $65 for a classic baby bearded dragon, with an older dragon, different colored, or morph, costing more. The cost to feed a baby bearded dragon is a little more than the cost of feeding an adult. For a baby, anticipate paying between $40 to $80 a month for insects and other food and around $50 for an adult bearded dragon. The monthly cost to feed a bearded dragon can significantly vary depending on what the current prices are and what you are buying. Lastly, you should expect to pay anywhere from $50 to $100 for a vet appointment, which varies depending on the location.

Misconception #4
Bearded dragons are mean and aggressive

By nature, bearded dragons are not mean or aggressive toward humans. For the minority of bearded dragons that display aggressive behaviors, owners can usually trace those behaviors to past trauma or abuse, poor diet, improper handling, illness, brumation, or stress. Contrarily, they are highly aggressive toward other lizards and can inflict significant injuries or even kill another dragon.

Addressing Concerns and Misconceptions

When uncertainty presents itself regarding your bearded dragon and its care, the best thing you can do is seek wise counsel. Find someone who can give you solid information and advice based on their deep understanding of bearded dragons and/or experience.

CHAPTER 10

Conclusion

Bearded dragons have numerous praiseworthy qualities that make caring for them and meeting their specialized requirements worthwhile. From their cute little facial expressions and amusing personalities to how easily they can be cared for and handled, they make rewarding long-term companions.

The Rewards of Bearded Dragon Ownership

The rewards of owning a bearded dragon are great. They make lovely companions, and their easygoing personalities make them enjoyable to interact with. Despite the challenges and learning curve that commonly accompany the ownership of an unfamiliar pet, most bearded dragon owners find the rewards overshadow any shortcomings.

Learning About and Interacting with a Unique Species

Bearded dragons are fun and exciting pets to learn about and interact with. One aspect that makes them so intriguing to people is that they are found on an entirely different continent. Another aspect that makes them

Photo Courtesy of Isaiah Helmer

Photo Courtesy of Mikayla Sullivan

unique is their prehistoric look, making interacting with them feel even more special. With the many activities and toys available for bearded dragons, interacting with them is always enjoyable.

Enjoying their Behavior and Development

Bearded dragons are captivating to watch, especially during their first year of life. They grow much quicker than expected, and in no time at all, they are 16 inches long or more. Additionally, they make great pets for people who want an interactive animal during the day. During the day, you can observe a bearded dragon become immersed in chasing its feeder insects, happily basking under its basking lamp, exploring, and climbing.

Providing a Good Quality of Life

Giving your bearded dragon a good quality of life separates a good pet owner from a poor one. As you provide the best life possible for your bearded dragon, your pet will reward you with unconditional love and companionship and give you a sense of purpose and responsibility.

Continued Learning and Resources

Keeping up with ever-changing technologies and information is vital to providing the best care possible for your lizard. There are many ways to stay up to date, and with the Internet at the tips of your fingers, it is nearly impossible to get left behind. Learning from various sources is one of the most effective ways to get a deeper understanding and an unbiased opinion about bearded dragons and their care.

FUN FACT
The Oldest Bearded Dragon

Bearded dragons have a lifespan of 10 to 15 years, although, with optimal care, some individuals have been known to live longer. For example, the oldest recorded bearded dragon, Sebastian, lived to be 18 years old in the UK. Sebastian was reportedly born on June 1, 1997, and died on January 24, 2015, making him 18 years and 237 days old at the time of his death. Various factors, including genetics, diet, and regular health care, can influence the life span of a bearded dragon.

Books

Rishon, Danny, Bearded Dragon Bible, Independently Published, 2022

De Vosjoli, Philippe, Robert Mailloux, Susan Donoghue, Roger Klingengerg, and Jerry Cole, Bearded Dragon Manuel 3rd Edition, CompanionHouse Book, 2022

Websites

Bearded Dragon.org
www.beardeddragon.org

This site is a great website that contains a ton of valuable information and a large community forum.

Reptile Advisor
www.reptileadvisor.com/baby-bearded-dragon-care/

This website is a free resource for reptile owners that offers many resources like weekly informational guides to help you give your bearded dragon the best care.

Josh's Frog
www.new.joshsfrogs.com

This website is a well-known and trusted company that delivers feeder insects to your front door at a fraction of the cost compared to other big-name pet stores.

Chewy
www.chewy.com

Chewy, Inc. is an excellent company that sells a wide range of pet food, including live insects and many other pet supplies, such as bearded dragon enclosures and equipment and decorations. They value their customers and are passionate about providing excellent customer service.

Association of Reptilian and Amphibian Veterinarians
www.arav.org

This is a valuable website to help bearded dragon owners find a qualified veterinarian close to home.

Reptiles Lounge
www.reptileslounge.com

This website is an online store dedicated to providing all things related to reptiles. They've got everything from enclosure items and decorations to food.

Photo Courtesy of Cole Ferris

Forums

www.beardeddragonforum.com
https://community.morphmarket.com

Other Resources

Reptiles Magazine
P.O. Box 6040
Mission Viejo, CA 92690
www.reptilesmagazine.com

Support and Advice from Other Owners and Experts

Attending reptile expos in your area is a great way to meet breeders and other passionate bearded dragon lovers. Expos are also excellent places to get trusted support and advice from the people there. Another way to get the help you need is by connecting with people through social media who have experience with bearded dragons. Don't forget that a veterinarian also serves as another resource for support and advice.

Staying Up To Date on the Latest Developments in Bearded Dragon Care and Husbandry

The more we have learned about the special care bearded dragons require, the better care we have been able to provide for them, especially over the last decade. Products and equipment to care for bearded dragons are continuously improving. Since we are perpetually learning and improving how to better care for them, staying updated on changes or improvements to their care or husbandry is vital.

Made in the USA
Las Vegas, NV
21 April 2024